Ashley!
Peace and
Keep doing what you do!

THROUGH THE EYES OF THE JUDGED
autobiographical sketches by incarcerated young men

TERRANCE TURNER

TUAN DANG

BEN PETERS

SIMEON TERRY

CHANG SAECHAO

JOHNATHAN SMITH

FLOYD GONZALEZ

JOHN PAUL

edited by Stephanie Guilloud

The following organizations provided funds for the publication and distribution of this book:

A Territory Resource, Seattle Washington

The Community Foundation, Olympia Washington

Teaching for Tolerance, Southern Poverty Law Center

Voices from the WTO Project, Olympia Washington

Credits

Cover photo and all digital photography by Holly Sheehan, tech support from Matt and Andy at Thinklab.

Back cover art by Johnathan Dowand Smith.

Poem by Johnathan Smith and Simeon Terry.

Layout and book design by Stephanie Guilloud.

This book is dedicated to the parents and families who do their best to provide emotional support through our struggles.

A special dedication to the spirits of the mothers who have passed away. Their love and support continues to inspire.

THE GATEWAY PROGAM INTRODUCES:

Getting Out
Staying Out

A Multimedia Education and Advocacy Project

Includes:

Music Performance

Public Presentations

Cultural Workshops

Sequel to *Through the Eyes of the Judged*

Formerly incarcerated youth will be available to speak, perform, and lead discussions about issues facing young people in the U.S. today.

Community organizations, schools, and juvenile institutions are encouraged to get involved in this project and schedule events with the Gateway Program.

Find out more and call the Gateway Program at (360) 867-6025 about this new project and the two books, *Through the Eyes of the Judged* and its follow-up companion *Getting Out/ Staying Out* (available 2003).

THE GATEWAY PROGRAM

The Gateway Program is an innovative partnership between The Evergreen State College in Olympia, Washington and Maple Lane School, a nearby juvenile institution. The program was developed in 1996 by Dr. Carol J. Minugh, Suzanne Cravey, and Ricardo Leyva-Puebla in response to the lack of educational and cultural opportunities in state juvenile facilities. Through classes, workshops, and mentor projects, the mission of the program is to strengthen notions of self through cultural awareness and empowerment.

Guided by the principles of participatory research, the program recognizes the knowledge and experience of incarcerated youth. Asked what their needs were, the young residents at Maple Lane identified their desire to learn about their cultural heritages and experience a real classroom for once. The Gateway classes and seminars encourage critical thinking, public speaking, reading and writing skills, and group facilitation. The program provides opportunities for Evergreen students to integrate their intellectual pursuits with a broader awareness of the real-life challenges that face people in their community. The program offers residents at Maple Lane an opportunity to earn high school or college credit while experiencing a collaborative learning environment. Facilitators also work with Maple Lane counselors to offer college counseling and preparation to interested residents.

The dedicated board of directors includes Carol Minugh, a Native American Studies professor at The Evergreen State College; Suzanne Cravey, former Cultural Programs Coordinator at Maple Lane School and current staff; Ricardo Leyva-Puebla, Director of Minority Affairs at Tacoma Community College; and Jerome Johnson, a staff member at a local private group home for juvenile offenders. Their work has steered this unique program through five successful years. The proceeds from this book will contribute to the sustainability of the Gateway Program. Funds will help create tuition scholarships so that Maple Lane residents may earn college credit at Evergreen.

ACKNOWLEDGMENTS

This book was a collaborative project at every stage. As editor, I built upon the invaluable work of many others. The Gateway Program Board deserves special recognition and acknowledgment. Carol Minugh and Suzanne Cravey envisioned this project and supported my work throughout the process. Carol's dedicated work has sustained this unique program over the years. Suzanne's work as Cultural Programs Coordinator at Maple Lane encouraged the residents to reflect on their experiences and expand their understanding of their place in the world. We also wish to thank Sandra Youngen, superintendent of Maple Lane School, and Dan Robertson, assistant superintendent, for their cooperation and support.

Steve Menter and Matt Walsh coordinated the original class that inspired the autobiographies. As Evergreen students, they participated in the weekly sessions for two quarters and responded to the residents' desire for more classes. They coordinated a second weekly session in spring quarter. Steve has continued to support the book project, my work, and the guys inside through his commitment to the Gateway Program.

We could not have produced this book without financial assistance and support. I want to thank the Evergreen Foundation as our fiscal sponsor and John McCann for his support in writing grants. The Community Foundation, A Territory Resource (ATR), and Teaching for Tolerance provided us with grant money to print and distribute the book. Many Evergreen students have volunteered their time and energy to raise funds for the program, and we thank them for their work. The Gloria Dei Lutheran Church and individual contributors have donated generously to the project over the years. Our sponsors provide the necessary resources to complete community projects like this one.

Thanks to Dan Leahy, Julia Allen, and Holly Sheehan for their support, ideas, encouragement, and energy.

TABLE OF CONTENTS

INTRODUCTION

STEPHANIE GUILLOUD

Institutionalized juveniles inhabit a unique space in popular consciousness. They are, at once, the most visible and invisible populations. Politicians build their careers on images of violent teenagers and use their mandatory minimums and 3-strikes policies to vault into office. Sensationalized media transforms teenagers into violent maniacs without hope of change, people without pasts or futures.

Incarcerated juveniles get erased and become invisible despite the spotlight. The spotlight lies. The details, context, and background of the accused remain unseen. They have mothers and sisters and brothers and histories. Their lives happen over days and months and years, and much of it happens behind a barbed wire fence. The US public ignores prisoners living, learning, and breathing inside concrete and chain link. Incarcerated peoples' lives are erased by a public and a politic that wants an easy answer to the difficult problem of crime.

Eight young men in Washington state invite you to see their lives through these autobiographies. They tell their stories from behind the wall and invite you to see beyond the false images and stereotypes. Listening to people when they talk and tell their lives is a lost art. With all the information that gets blasted at us through TV, film, and radio, people have forgotten how to listen. These guys tell me about robberies and drugs and guns. They tell me about cops and trials and jail. They tell me about being young in Thailand, growing up on a reservation, or in a neighborhood in Spokane. These stories are not finished because the authors are young and changing every day. Their memories and life experiences up to this point glitter with detail and pound with powerful truth. The stories are their bones, their hands, their eyes. It is a gift to read them. Publishing these life stories is in direct resistance to the silence imposed by corporate media images, political agendas, and those tall metal doors that swing shut and slam.

What is crime?

The kids at Maple Lane were convicted of crimes that vary from drug offenses and burglary to assault, rape, and murder. They were convicted in a court and sentenced according to the law. That's a fact. Is it a fact that the justice system tried them with full access to just and due process? Not so sure. Are all the rapists, thieves, and drug-users behind these bars? Certainly not. Does the conviction rate of rapists, thieves, and drug-users with a little more cash flow differ in comparison with the conviction rate of rapists, thieves, and drug-users with no lawyer, no parent, no fall-back plan? Most assuredly, yes. People with money go home. People without money go to jail. Who commits crime? The facts of crime begin to blur with the more elusive reality of who goes to prison and why.

My proof lies in my own experience. After going to a large public junior high, my parents offered me the option of attending a competitive private high school. For better or worse, I chose to transfer. Switching from a racially diverse middle school of all learning levels to a carpeted, mostly white private school did not decrease the rate of crime around me. Getting high before school is not solely a ghetto phenomenon. Guys at my college prep school injected oranges with 100 proof grain alcohol and sucked on them before class. Teachers and parents used racist images of a dark stranger raping young girls to terrify us, but I was more afraid of being raped at the wrong party from a guy who always got what he wanted. I was friends with kids doing drugs. It wasn't a big deal. Would they have stolen for their habit? Hard to tell. They didn't have to. They already drove nice cars, bought as much weed as they liked, wore nice clothes - all this courtesy of birth. They didn't steal cause they were rich. They didn't get caught or go down cause they were white and rich, a very powerful combo. If they did get caught, they didn't go to any barbed wire school for "juvenile life" sentences. These kids I grew up with weren't labeled "delinquents" or "stupid" or "violent" or "superpredators." They were regular teenagers going through "phases" - maybe tagged as "rebels." Not so different from the guys at Maple Lane. Funny, full of ego and jokes, thinking a lot, not thinking at all. Teenage kids.

The difference between the two is major, though. Some have choices that look like - go to college and work for Dad, go to college and find a better job, travel to South America, or travel to Europe. The other kids, the guys at Maple Lane and other facilities, have choices that look like - protection with weapons or death, no food or stolen food, racist enemies or gangster friends. I grew up with choices, and I stare the difference in the face every time I walk in and out of Maple Lane. I taste and smell the details of a place and its laws whose fundamental purpose is to keep me and these guys separated.

By looking closely at their lives and looking closely at myself, I find out that crime is not an objective, universal truth but a manipulated lie bent and twisted to define who is good and who is bad. Who creates the definitions? People like the ones I went to high school with, all grown up. People with power, people with privilege, people who make decisions, not only for themselves but also for others. I do not exclude myself from this category. Nor do I exclude myself from the criminal classification. I just haven't been caught yet.

What is responsibility?

A white woman in her late twenties asks me a casual question. "What do you do?"

"I work with incarcerated teenage guys. They're writing their autobiographies. I'm editing them," I tell her. She asks if I am scared to go in there. I say no. She finishes the conversation, "I'm sure they've got tough lives. But at some point, they've got to take responsibility for their actions. Right?"

I don't answer.

These kids are locked away for months or many years. They write about the crimes that put them there. The juvenile justice system has defined them by their crimes, by that single incident. They begin to define themselves by their crimes or as criminals, yet they are commanded to take responsibility for their choices beneath the weight of their constant captivation. The weight of that one choice, that crime that led them to incarceration, surrounds them like the air they breathe. Responsibility is a rather good concept. Personal responsibility for particular choices helps one make better decisions when faced with future choices, or so I hear. But who will take responsibility for the particular sets of choices that face these kids? Before they are sent there and once they are released?

The staff on the inside and the attitude on the outside badgers them to take responsibility for their actions. Why them and not others? Do the men who commit crimes on a global scale take responsibility for their acts of violence and oppression? Has Charles Keating, the Savings and Loan thief who stole more money than the kids at Maple Lane can even imagine, taken responsibility for his crimes? Are these teenagers also responsible for the conditions that created their set of choices? Are they responsible for the fate of Southeast Asian immigrants that come to this country facing unbelievable odds? Are they personally responsible for the legislation that cuts support to single mothers, responsible for the poverty that was systematically forced on indigenous people on reservations?

This project strives to print the raw expressions of incarcerated young men and share them with folks who do not often see their experiences represented. People of color, poor people, youth, and incarcerated people (among many others) are not allowed space in the literary world to tell their lives or stories as they choose. As an editor, I worked with the writers and their texts to create a book that honestly documents their stories and also challenges the white, middle class ideas of acceptable writing. Steve Menter wrote about his experience as an Evergreen State College student working with Maple Lane students. Julia Allen wrote a chapter that provides some facts and analysis about the juvenile justice system in Washington state and the U.S. We hope that our work, as young people on the outside, provides context and stimulates continued work with prison populations. This book, though, is undeniably theirs - Simeon's, Johnathan's, Floyd's, Ben's, Tuan's, Terrance's, John's, and Chang's.

Through the Eyes of the Judged offers an amazing opportunity to share the stories of people who have lived through hell and haven't yet hit 21. It also offers an opportunity to question the fundamental system that creates the cycles of poverty, crime, and imprisonment.

DIRECTOR'S NOTE

CAROL J. MINUGH
DIRECTOR OF THE GATEWAY PROGRAM

*"Our main job is to keep the boys safe from
themselves and from others."*

This statement comes from the staff at Maple Lane. The lack of
resources has continually reduced the opportunities for state institutions to emphasize rehabilitation. Along with cutbacks in funding, the
number of incarcerated youth who have mental disabilities has increased dramatically. Society often fails to address these problems when
children enter the education system, much less when they are born.
Children born to a substance abusing parent are prime candidates for
incarceration from the time of their birth. It is not hard to identify
these youth within the system.

Profiling, whether it is racial or by the neighborhood they come
from, is a barrier many of these youth have faced within the school
system. When they enter a class they are seen as potential trouble.
They then often become what is expected of them. To turn this around
means they have to work twice as hard as most of the students to
achieve acceptance and proceed to academic excellence. At the very
first meeting of the Gateway program, we brought Evergreen students and Maple Lane youth together and asked "what we as an educational group could possibly do." One answer that sticks with me
today is: "I just want to be in a regular classroom once in my life."
This statement is reflective of many of the youth at Maple Lane.

Some would say putting students in special education classes gives
them a better chance of success, while others would say it solidifies the

idea that they are dumb. When a major population of a specific race, neighborhood, or tribal group is in special education, we have profiling at a very young age. It is little wonder that these young people are in trouble later in their lives.

The values of our materialistic society are devastating to those who don't have access to resources. The well-being of the nation is measured by economic growth and depends upon the population accumulating more and more goods. Prestige is measured by how much we have. This pressure leaves many of our young people looking for ways they can be a part of this accumulating society. The avenues open to them are limited and those most accessible are often illegal.

In the Gateway Program, we see youth who receive their first real help within the institution. One young man was convicted for running guns for a militant group. At age 13, he had a child but could not get a job to support this child. Being in the institution allowed him to work and gain a vocation so that he could send money to the mother for the support of the child. He believes that if he was not arrested and institutionalized he, in all likelihood, would have become much more deeply involved in criminal activity. Others report that they get "three squares and a bed" as a positive from being incarcerated. It seems there is something wrong with this. There are many people out there who will prey on young people who have no resources. You might argue that our Social Welfare system addresses these needs, but many of these youth have adult responsibilities from the time they are able to walk. Becoming a dependent child again is a near impossibility. As is turning against their parents, as we will see in the stories.

I do not want to leave you with the impression that all of the youth who are incarcerated are from disadvantaged homes. The population at Maple Lane comes from all walks of life, albeit fewer come from stable homes. The following questions are critical to our justice system: Is a child less likely to be incarcerated if their parents can afford adequate defense? Is there racial profiling in our judicial system? Is a racial minority likely to receive a tougher sentence than a majority youth? It is our hope that you will critically consider these questions. Ask yourself what is happening in your community.

We lock these children away and hope that the punishment will help them to decide to become productive members of our society. Unfortunately 80 - 90 % of these youth will be repeat offenders. The

High Schools within the institutions work with students who have not been able to succeed in other schools. The teachers try to motivate them and attempt to address the many years of educational neglect. Many of the youth have learning disabilities. Others are extremely bright. Those students who are motivated and bright graduate from high school or obtain a GED. What then? There is no funding for higher education for incarcerated youth. Federal laws prohibit these youth from receiving any financial assistance from federal financial aid. State aid is also not available to them. In fact, the bright minds are put on hold until they are released. Do they become the most capable criminals or do they find more acceptable uses for their creative talents?

The Gateway Program is one way to address this question. Recognizing the capabilities of the youth and strengthening their abilities to think critically and analyze complex information is a critical part of the program, as is financial assistance for tuition. The program works to build within the youth the ability and confidence to succeed within higher education. We don't think that we have all of the answers, but we believe in the importance of self-esteem based on achievement. This book is a part of their achievement. It was not easy for them to share themselves with us, but they did. This is their writing, telling their stories in their own words.

INCARCERATION
TERRANCE TURNER

We are all imprisoned. The only difference is the circumstance of each person's individual incarceration. Whether a person can become conscious of his imprisonment depends solely on self.

On the 17th of December, 1994, I found myself mixed up in a crime that would change the course of my life forever. If ever asked what really happened that night, I have chosen to catch convenient amnesia. It's a part of my life I regret and wish to forget.

The following Monday I was arraigned on charges of first degree kidnapping, first-degree robbery and attempted murder. A legal technicality would not permit me and my co-defendants to have the same public defender for legal representation. There was only one public defender for Pierce County at the time, so the state was required to hire a private attorney for me. If it weren't for this legal technicality, I would have lost my decline hearing since my family didn't have the funds to provide sufficient representation for my case. A decline hearing is where the decision is made whether a juvenile will be "declined" out of the juvenile system. Then the only other option would be a trial in adult court, being tried as an adult. If declined within the juvenile system, the plan was to start me out at a maximum-security prison in Shelton.

In that situation, my maximum sentence range was a minimum of 20 years to life in a state penitentiary. At age fifteen, I feared the possibility of spending one-fifth of my life in captivity in a place where an inmate's personal safety is a secondary concern. The prosecuting attorney offered me a plea bargain. The state would drop the kidnap and an additional POSP (possession of stolen property) charge that had been added to the other charges along the way. But first I had to agree to a manifest justice, which means accepting a longer sentence than is usually allowed in the juvenile system, and plead guilty to first-degree assault and first-degree robbery.

My mother had little to do with the decision making. Our relationship had been severed by my recalcitrant behavior over the past year. I weighed the few options that I had been offered on the broken scales of justice: 20 years to life in prison if I went against the grain, tried to fight it, took it to trial and cost the state more money or... agree to just under six years in a juvenile institution if I "just made things a lot easier on myself." I took the plea bargain, hoping I was "just making things a lot easier on myself." On March 23, 1995, I was shackled and put on state transportation. Our destination was Maple Lane School, a juvenile institution in Centralia, Washington.

Butterflies in my stomach turned into swarming bees stinging the inside walls. It felt like everything was in slow motion as the vehicle sped down the off ramp on 1-5. I stared at my surroundings as I had never done before, as they blurred by. I tried to implant the littlest details knowing how long it would be before I would see these things again.

The view approaching the institution reminded my of those little desktop ornaments that have a small town in a glass ball, you shake it and the glittery snow swirls around and slowly falls on the houses. Looking at Maple Lane, I saw a small town trapped behind a chain link fence. The transportation vehicle was admitted into this mini-fortress, and it drove to a tan brick building I later found out was the facility's clinic.

My first day as an inmate at Maple Lane School. I was escorted inside the building and told to strip in front of two security guards who reminded my of Siskel and Ebert from their weight differentiation. I was given a navy blue coverall uniform, shower thongs, and underwear. I was then handed a board that read in bright white letters - name, Terrance Turner - age, 15, Date of Birth 8-23-79. I held it up to my chest while they took front and profile pictures.

Within the confines of these gates I've had constant homesickness and semi-states of what feels like temporary insanity from the chaotic atmosphere. I've had to accept the stress and the anger. The state is holding my mother accountable financially for my incarceration, including my room and board. The amount she pays is based on her income. For victim restitution, she was sued for more than $2000. Her wages have been garnished. This is just part of what makes me angry about the system and brings my human tolerance level to the boiling point.

Incarceration has altered me physically and mentally. My skin seems pale and my body, narrow. According to national standards and requirements, we are provided with adequate and balanced nutrition. Still there are times that if my good sense doesn't reject the food on the tray by refusing it, then my stomach will. There are times when my mind becomes entwined like thick sticker bushes with mixed emotions and thoughts that can't be untangled . . . thoughts I can only block out for so long. There's no way to fix or mend the imbalance being created by my so-called rehabilitation.

Tattooed on my upper right arm are seven names of close friends in remembrance to their existence and our friendship. They're all dead now. Of the seven, six were shot to death. Four of the six were shot by a friend. Two were shot by rivals, and one was stabbed to death. If I was out there during the time I've been incarcerated, I would probably be dead like them.

Everyday in this country, 10 American children ages 18 and under are killed nationwide in gun accidents, suicides, and homicides. Many more are severely wounded or maimed. There is no doubt in my mind that if I was out there in the midst of all these tragedies, one of the names of the souls on my arm would have eventually been my own.

Once you're in the system, you become trapped. You become part of the very walls that trap you. It's like falling through a thin layer of ice on a lake. When you fall through the ice, you fall into an underwater world of the unknown. Your body immediately goes into shock. The freezing water stabs at your skin like a million needles. Your first reaction is to get back to the surface. Swimming in the direction of freedom, you kick your legs as hard as you can. But the water slows your movement and the light you find when you reach the surface isn't as inviting as you expected when you see it through the thick layer of ice sealing you in. You pound on the ice, but the ice is strong and doesn't give way to your weak attempt to break its walls. You instinctively gasp for air allowing a river of frigid water to rush into your lungs.

A huge air exchange bubble floats to the surface only to find itself trapped . . . as trapped as you are. You might know this in the corporate world as the "glass ceiling." I know it as incarceration.

Society is quick to land its children in prisons and institutions. Society is quick to pass new laws to keep its children in captivity. From in here, it's like standing on one side of a two-way mirror, where you can't see your own reflection. Try looking at it from this side of the razor wire . . . try surviving . . . and see why most children who are incarcerated become repeat offenders when they're released.

Incarceration leaves no room for sympathy. If you want to survive then you must prove yourself physically and mentally. You must be fit enough to pass every test thrown at you by the other inmates. You can't just do your time and get out. It's not that simple. You have two choices . . . become the victim or the victimizer. What would you choose? Because in reality, there is no in-between.

I have it better than most of the guys in here. Some are insane from the so-called rehabilitation efforts of the juvenile justice system. Some are dead - their choice: suicide. There are those that never get visits because their family either doesn't care or has disowned them. Some families live too far away or don't have reliable transportation to come visit them. Some never get phone calls or mail. I am fortunate because my mother makes the hour drive from Tacoma every Sunday to visit me.

I grew up knowing my father only by a few photographs of him in the family photo album. It's not uncommon to be raised in a single parent family. According the the US census bureau, 60% of children being born in our country today will be living in single parent families by the time they are 18 years old. In my case, my mother was lonely, and my brother and I were fatherless. A single income was not enough to support our family of three.

Before I knew it, I had a replacement father figure . . . a new stepfather. I hated him, and my brother shared the feeling. It was like living in a jail. When my brother and I were gone, my stepfather would search through our personal stuff and confiscate things he thought unsuitable. When we were there he would yell at us and interrogate us. Sometimes it got violent. At some point, my step-dad brought a gun into the house. He told my mother the reason he bought the gun was because he was afraid of my brother and me. I can only assume my mother accepted this reasoning because she allowed the gun to stay in the house. . . which she had vowed she would never do.

Shortly after this, my mother found a gun that I had brought into the house. At the time she found it, I was already in juvenile detention. About a week after I got out, an argument with my step-dad escalated and the next thing you know he was running down the stairs. When he came up the stairs he had in his hand a .357 pistol grip.

"Either one of you mother f—ers eva' pull a gun on me, I got somethin' fo' yo' ass!"

The weekend after my mother had found my gun, she came to visit me. It was Mother's Day, which only added to the grief. She broke down emotionally at the beginning of the visit. Through wet cheeks and sniffles she asked me, "Why do both my sons have to be locked up on Mother's Day? Don't you care about me? Do you do this on purpose? Didn't I raise you and your brother good enough?"

It was a barrage of questions that I couldn't dodge. I was riddled with bullets of guilt that pierced my heart for an eternity.

What puzzled me the most was the fact that my mother had not even bothered to ask me where I had gotten the gun in the first place. She wouldn't have been surprised to find out where I had found the gun - a .380 Loricen 8 shot, 7 in the clip, one in the chamber. I found it at Lakeview Elementary School - in the schoolyard - by the fence - loaded.

Once again, the incandescent floodlights shatter the shadowy symetrics of my roughly 6' by 9' cell when it's lights out. It's Friday night. There hasn't been any sign of snow this January. Instead, showering raindrops have baptized the uneven, discolored grass and cracked concrete, allowing puddles to become small ponds and sidewalks to become mild current rivers. Twelve intimidating feet of steel-strength chain link fence decorated with hundreds of yards of spiraling razor wire quickly eradicates any hope or attempt of forgetting where I've been evaporating over the past four years. For every day of the year, there is a brick in this cell that secures the absence of my freedom. There are exactly 365 of them. How do I know? I've counted them.

The pale incandescent light, for most inmates, crushes any possibility of sleep without blankets over their heads, and reflects a gloomy glow off the 14" by 8" off-white bricks. The pale light casts a multitude of soft shadows, proving itself sufficient for writing.

Fully clothed, goose bumps populate the epidermis of my skin, elevating the almost invisible hairs on my arms. A Lionel Richie CD that seeps out of the speakers in my radio is now in competition with an unwanted musical Mother Nature is playing. A live performance of rain collides with the aluminum gutters of the building and creates an indescribable annoyance.

The powerful beam of a flashlight has just interrupted the already disturbed peace of isolation, for the purpose of a "head count" which takes place every hour on the hour. Common courtesy is not a favored practice in this mini-penitentiary. This explains why the yelling in the cell parallel to mine goes unacknowledged, leaving those who can sleep without consideration.

Three vertical steel bars in front of my window forces my vision into grid-like sections. Each section portrays the environment as segregated and artificial. An unknown darkness engulfs the mysterious frontier that lies on the other side of the fence.

We are all imprisoned. The only difference is the circumstance of each person's individual incarceration. Whether a person can become conscious of his imprisonment depends solely on self. Societies of our past and present have given its children the worst kind of imprisonment. Society has imprisoned the thought-process of its children allowing these children to grow up as if they were autistic adults. . . . setting too many limits on themselves . . . limits society has imposed.

When the word prison, penitentiary, detention center, institution, correctional facility, and incarceration are heard most minds automatically think - bars, gates, razor wire, shackles, and guard towers. Most, if not all, of these words represent an absence of freedom, but it doesn't mean we aren't incarcerated without them. Religion, media, and schools are major contributors to all forms of mental imprisonment. Any time you are without freedom of choice, you are incarcerated. By imprisonment of thought, subliminal restraints have been set in the conscious of society's children. Most of you are blind to that . . . maybe that's because it would hurt too much to see.

I woke up in a box today, and realized that I've lived in a box for the last nineteen years. For the past four years, I've lived in a more confined box that society better knows as a jail . . . institution or penitentiary. Inside this box, I live in an even smaller box called a cell that exists only to suppress, justified by law. My box is fifteen steps by nine steps, heel to toe. I wear a size nine. You do the math.

This box is painted beige with a linoleum floor. There is a window at the back of my box that allows an abundance of light to pour into the box and reflect off of the walls, further illuminating my situation.

This window can be a window of either happiness or dismay. Sometimes I like looking out the window. I can see the surrounding town and its every movement. But sometimes when I look out the window I can't help but see the twelve-foot chain link fence decorated with double bladed razor wire held in place with concrete reinforcements and steel poles. This sight can trigger an unwanted reminder of how much I hate where I am and how much hate I possess for those who keep me here . . . kept here without freedom of any sort.

There is another window on the door of my box. This window is severely scratched and about the size of a business envelope square. This window allows a foggy view of the other side of my box and allows me to see the villain that feeds me through the folding tray door about a foot under the window. There is a sink-toilet contraption at the front of my box that allows no room for privacy. It has the appearance of a New York subway urinal. It leaves a stale aroma of urine and other excrement that drifts up through the contraption orifices.

There aren't any temperature control apparatuses that control the climate in my box. My comfort or discomfort is in someone else's control. This leaves me freezing in the winter with two paper-thin blankets. In the summer these blankets double as curtains to block the light and heat that engulfs the room.

What I have described is only a fragment of my hell. My life. My death. My box. The world, as I view it, is a series of boxes entwined within each other so intricately that it becomes hard to see. These boxes we're not aware of depict our future and our children's future by setting limitations on our destiny. Today my box is jail. Tomorrow, who knows? The world is a box we're born in with no escape except for the box we all leave in - called a coffin.

I solely believe that my environment was the major contributor to my present reality. Society promotes materialism . . . and society not only promotes violence, society glorifies it. The US history book that is required for high school is filled with wars and acts of violence that formed the foundation for the American economy today. This leaves most to believe that violence is acceptable . . . and if it is not acceptable, why glorify it?

Places like this is where I've been deteriorating for the past four years. Coming here I've lost a chunk of my life and part of myself. I've lost the opportunity to get my first minimum wage job and graduate with my Class of '97. I lost the chance to grow up like a normal teenager.

Some have told me, "Look at the bright side. While you were in here you earned your GED and high school diploma." But if given the chance to achieve these things in a positive atmosphere, I could have achieved those academics no matter where I was.

Incarceration should be for the system that incarcerates, not for kids who have made mistakes in life. The system that founds the infrastructure of the penal systems should be held accountable for what they create . . . they create repeat offenders by putting them through a crash course, "HOW TO BE A CRIMINAL 101." That's what we're learning inside the gates of these institutions and prisons. They're allowing minds of innocence to be corrupted by hopeless convicts and career criminals. I take full responsibility for my actions that December night. If there were a way to rewind the hands of time, I wouldn't be where I am today. If I would have had a better understanding of choice and the insignificance of materialism, I could have easily chosen a different direction in life.

This is no place to grow up.

My first week at Green Hill, (another Juvenile facility) this guy gave me this book *Malcolm X: The Autobiography.* He said, "Here, read this." I pushed the book back in his face and said, "You read it." But when I ended up in lock up, what else did I have to do? So I read it.

A common question asked today is, 'Why do children grow up so violent and aggressive?' And my response to that question is, ask yourself. What can you expect when children mirror their environment? Early childhood through the pre-adolescent stage in child development is when a child learns easily and rapidly.

When two little kids hit on each other with a toy, it isn't out of instinct. It is a learned reaction to get what they want and is triggered by what they have seen. Arcades are swamped with video games that sever heads, rip out spines, massacre people, and more. Cartoons are filled with guns and violence. Impressionable young children watch as a person or animal is shot. Then they just get up and walk away, teaching children a sense of invincibility.

I began to notice around the age of 10 that my brother and I were at extreme opposites. I realized he would do the damnedest things to make me furiously burn with the words, "I hate you!" at the tip of my tongue. Sometimes those very words would indeed shove their way to the forefront. "He don't care about me!" I would absentmindedly retort in arguments with my mother when I was infuriated with my brother and his antics. She would always try to comfort me with condoling words of encouragement. "You two only fight all the time cause you love each other so much," she would tell me.

One Saturday night I ran into my brother and his wife at the movie theater in the mall. And it sure as hell didn't seem like he 'loved' me very much then. I approached him jokingly, shooting him in the face with a toy gun that harmlessly shot colorful plastic capsules.

My brother grew instantly furious and told me, "Boy! You keep playing with those fake guns, you're gonna get shot for real!" I laughed at his remark and told him he was overreacting, showing off for his wife.

I've always wondered what my brother thought when he found out that less than 10 minutes after he told me that, I did, indeed, get shot 'for-real'! Getting shot had nothing to do, however, with the toy gun I had whimsically been armed with earlier. Especially since, if memory serves me right, my brother destroyed the harmless toy in a fit of anger.

It was a frightening experience to walk out of the mall with five of my closest friends - a harmless pack of eighth graders, give or take a few seventh graders, and desperately have to dodge life-threatening bullets as they whizzed and whistled by our ears in an unprovoked drive-by.

Our group of six quickly dispersed haphazardly, frantically in search of immediate refuge. A friend and I managed to stay together briefly and found safety by laying adjacent to an 'island' in the mall's parking lot.

After hearing our assailants' tires screech off in the distance, we jumped up and attempted to seek shelter inside the mall. That's when I discovered I had collided with one of the bullets that had wickedly danced from the staccato fiery flashes of a small chrome semi-automatic handgun. A .380 hollow tip bullet had scheduled unexpected travel arrangements through muscle and tissue in my lower right leg, leaving two holes in my flesh, searing my skin.

A car emerged out of what seemed like nowhere and offered us a ride to St. Claire Hospital. Without delay we accepted the offer and were on our way to the hospital. We arrived in minutes that left the lasting effect of a 'timeless forever.' My friend helped me limp through the 'Emergency Entrance.' Once inside, we were immediately separated. My friend quickly disappeared as I was put on a stretcher and whisked away down the crowded hallways of the hospital where my stretcher was parked next to a dead person. If he wasn't dead, he sure did look it!

I kept thinking to myself, 'Don't cry! Be strong! Don't die!' After a brief eternity, some hospital personnel in starched, stark-white over-coats came over and cut my clothes off with an awkward pair of medical scissors, repeatedly asking me if I was 'hurt anywhere else.'

I was wheeled into a room where I was unnecessarily interrogated and harassed by local police, simultaneously receiving medical attention. My mother quickly came to the rescue after the hospital called her and briefed her on the situation. Over the annoying static that crackled from one of the officers' police radios, I learned that I wasn't the only one who had been shot in the incident. I immediately panicked. I kept asking who was shot and if they would be all right. The officer proved to be a 'consistent' asshole, refusing to tell me anything. I later found out that it was one of our original six who had been shot. He suffered two wounds, but fortunately, they were in the leg area, proving to be far from life-threatening.

The following Monday I went to school, hobbling on crutches, and was an instant celebrity. I soon found out that 'getting shot' and surviving made you 'cool.' It gave you status. I enjoyed the spotlight while I had it.

After getting shot and becoming a small-time celebrity, I slowed down a lot. I didn't hang out as much and stayed home a lot more. Sadly, it didn't last long. After a while I started rationalizing that I didn't just get shot. I survived! That if I wasn't invincible, I was the next best thing. And that decision, based on the choices I had or chose to accept, changed the course of my life forever.

I had gotten my hands on a few real guns before this incident, but only to be cool. It made me a 'man.' I started carrying a weapon with different intentions. Now I needed to carry a gun for personal protection . . . for survival.

Why does a thirteen-year-old kid need protection? And mostly, why does a thirteen-year-old need a gun to protect himself? Who is supposed to be protecting kids these days? Good questions. But why shouldn't we need to carry a gun to protect ourselves from assailants who shoot at us for unknown reasons? Why shouldn't we carry weapons, when people that attempted to take a future are still free to make a second attempt? Why are thirteen year-old kids being left defenseless to the dangers of ill-natured people in society? These are the questions you need to be asking yourselves.

It is strange to completely understand the complicated layers of misdirection in attempting to solve some of America's worst problems. As for me, my problem is my current incarceration and that everything in my life has contributed to this, directly or indirectly.

I've been incarcerated for four years and counting. In these last six months of my incarceration at Maple Lane, I've made a remarkable effort to change. And I have changed. But if I fail to revert, then I will become prey to the predators inside these gates. Predators that feed off weakness. This inner struggle for freedom exists inside these gates and most institutions like it. So my question is, Where's the possibility for rehabilitation when it's not possible to submit to it without putting yourself in harm's way? How do you win in a no-win situation?

In conclusion, it is evident that I would not be who I am today if it weren't for the decisions I made, based on the choices I had and/or chose to see. Nor would you be the person you are today without traveling the road you've traveled. That's what makes us individuals by virtue.

I have tried to put emphasis on the importance of decisions and the basic scientific law of 'Cause and Effect.' Causes and effects originate and manifest from the decisions we make and are influenced by the choices we're exposed to in the course of our lives.

I've tried to emphasize that decisions need to be made carefully and that the choices we confront should be analyzed thoroughly. Failure to analyze these choices can allow you to unconsciously overlook choices that you weren't aware of, thus causing you to make irrational decisions. Decisions that directly and/or indirectly alter the course of your life permanently.

I am aware that there are many alternative paths my life could have traveled, including death, based on the decisions I made. But I am content with the roads I've traveled, for they have brought me to the present. A beautiful present and renovated image of self and thought that started with change.

Terrance's autobiography is a combination of work he completed with an Evergreen student and Gateway volunteer, Sandra Smith, and his work in the autobiography class. Sandra worked with Terrance over a period of months to write down the stories and details of his experience. The residents in the autobiography class were inspired by the work Sandra and Terrance did to write their own stories.

TRUTH

TUAN NGOC DANG

My first accomplishment was getting my high school diploma. This gave me the thought that I could do anything in life if I want it bad enough. I was the first one in my family that ever graduated from high school. It's easy to say I could do anything. Now I'm at a point that I understand everything in my life is a struggle.

The first memory I have is full of pain, beatings, whippings and being scared. This is all I know. If I picked up a rice bowl wrong, I was beaten. If I lost my shoes, I was beaten. If my brother lost my shoes, I was beaten. I live in a family of six, two older brothers, one younger sister, and a mom and dad, of course. My family is from Vietnam. I am a full-blooded Vietnamese. We came over to America because we didn't want to deal and live in the land of communist.

My earliest memory is in California at the age of two. It was a hot summer day when I was crying for attention. That got me into some trouble, and I ended up in the garbage. My dad, being crazy like the guy he is, got angry with my crying and decided to put me in the garbage. Now this is not the regular kind of garbage that can only carry one hefty bag, this was one of those big five-foot tall by seven-foot wide garbage dumpsters. I was in there for about an hour or so when an old Vietnamese friend found me and decided to take care of me. My dad managed to find out where I was and came and got me about a week later. He was scared for me. Our family made up. Then it was all fun and games.

Growing up in a Vietnamese family and environment was very violent. Everything was taken out through kicks and punches. I can still remember my uncles and my dad got into a little rumble at my grandpa's house in California. My uncle got his balls smashed and my dad was running around fighting and punching everyone. It was crazy. All I remember hearing was them screaming and yelling "*Du Ma Mie*" this in my native language means 'mother fucker.' My brothers and I was in the back room watching a Lakers vs Sonics game. I can still remember I was rooting for the Sonics saying "hurry, catch up" and then I would laugh about it because I also thought that catch up means ketchup, as in French fries. I was so use to the violence and having violence in my family that the fighting that went on outside didn't bother me one bit. Cause I was either getting beat up at home or my brothers were.

My father is a very strong alcoholic and weed addict. I think he had this behavior introduced to him when we came to America. We lived in a big apartment complex in California. I remember Dad use to come home and would go straight to one of his Mexican friend's houses. Sometimes I would come along just because he would bring me along. When I was there, I remember this one Mexican guy drew me a picture of a revolver gun. They just sat there and smoked weed, laughed, and had a great time. Every time I would come over he would draw me a gun, all of them different. It all looked nice to me. After coming home from their house, my dad would open up our coffee table and pull out some weed to smoke. When he is either high or sober, he's the nicest person. He can make you laugh and put a smile on your face when you are feeling down. Back in our country and in California, he use to play in a Vietnamese band. He was the drummer guitarist and a singer. He would sing in Vietnamese to the American people and would just make them smile. He has that special expression that no one can miss. But when he gets drunk and you aren't family you are an enemy to him. He use to tell me stories about when he was in the war back in Vietnam. That he witnessed his own family members get killed right in front of him. He told me one time the Viet Cong communists of North Vietnam had got into an argument with one of our family members and during the confrontation, he got killed. My dad got so mad when he heard about it that he wanted to go to the V.Cs and confront them. My grandpa and uncles told him no, and if he did that, they would probably get killed too. They held him back, and he got so mad that he went inside the house and decided to chop off one of his fingers in respect and anger. He did it, too. He cut his own pinkie off and threw it at my grandpa. He now only has half a finger on one of his hands.

Coming to America was very difficult for our family. It was a big change yet a big struggle for our family. It was better, in a way, out of the communist land but I know it was hard to leave our whole family behind. One of the things that I hate about America is that the system is corrupted, not saying ours wasn't. The main complaint is that in my culture beating your child is right and beating your wife is also right. But when my mom and dad would get into some arguments - they usually get into some fist to fist combat - then the neighbor would hear and call the police. My father got arrested for domestic violence many times. I don't think it really mattered much to him. It is in our blood too deep to just let it go because the police and law tells him so. Our family has too much pride.

We would celebrate Vietnamese holidays, use Vietnamese food and remedies to cure our sickness. We never used any Tylenol or American medicine. Basically we lived Little Saigon in Big America. Being a Vietnamese kid in America was never too hard for me at this point in my life. California, especially L.A., was mainly mixed culture. I never had no one make any racial slurs towards me. I remember taking the school bus to school one day and this one white kid was talking shit to me. As soon as we got off of the bus, I ran towards him and beat him up. Ever since I did that the neighborhood and school kids would call me little Bruce Lee. At this point I was about four years old. My brother Hoa was four years older than I was, my brother Quy was the oldest, he was six year older than I was. I also have a younger sister her name is Thuy, and she is one year younger than me.

We ended up moving because my parents would get into bad fights. We would get kicked out. Now I remember living with my uncle in San Jose. He was cool. My dad would always come over to his restaurant and snort some cocaine with his friends. One time I went in the restroom to go take a piss. I caught one of my dad's friends standing there rolling up a dollar bill like a straw to snort some coke. These guys were like big time Vietnamese Ballers (mafia, big timers). They always wore nice clothes. My dad once told me that his friends a long time ago would smuggle pounds and pounds of coke to America from Vietnam through the plane and use babies. They would cut open babies' stomachs and stuff them with the cocaine. Then they would carry the baby over the plane and play it off like the baby would be asleep. When the whole time they was smuggling the coke over. I guess money is more important to some people. It's funny things people do for money.

We moved again to Van Nuys. We stayed there for a while. The reason why we moved so much is because my dad is an alcoholic. Mom didn't like it, and they would always fight. Everyone would kick us out. I remember one day my dad had just gotten off of work and was hungry. He said in English to my mom "Go in the bathroom and turn on the bath," so she did. When he was ready to take a shower, they got into a big argument over which one is called the shower and which one is the bath. My dad thought that the bottom faucet was called the shower and the top one was called the bath. My mom thought that the top was called the shower and the bottom one was called the bath. She was right. They was arguing about that subject for awhile. All I remember was my dad pulling out my mom's hair. My mom broke the toilet with a hammer out of anger. Dad got even more angry and beat her up even more. Mom got mad and picked up a knife and stabbed my dad in the ribs. Their fight started in the bathroom and went to the other side of our apartment. Our neighbor saw and decided to call the police.

Mom and Dad was both arrested. A policeman told me, my brothers, and sister to come with him. I got scared and asked the police men -Where were we going? He looked at me and said -Around. I looked at him and said - Around like the roller coaster? We all laughed, and he ended up taking us with him. Hoa and I went one way. They took my brother Quy and my sister Thuy somewhere else. I remember them taking us to this one house where there was a lot of kids. Everyone was speaking English, and we could barely understand them. I remember playing with some legos and I saw this little girl lego. It made me think about my little sister. We started crying. I didn't know if we was ever going to see her again. Months went by and our family got back together again.

We moved to Sacramento. I remember Mom and Dad got into another fight. This time it was over some alcohol. Mom never liked Dad drinking so she asked him to choose the beer or her. My dad didn't understand how she could ask him to choose a human being over a bottle of beer - it was no kind of comparison. Dad, of course, said beer, just cause. So they got into it again. He went out right after to buy some beer just so it would get her mad. When he got home, Mom locked him out. Out of anger, he punched through the window and broke it letting himself in and cut his hand doing it during the process. When he got in they was fist fighting for awhile, then my mom decided to pick up two knives and started to swerve it around in front of her saying to my father if he wanted some then just jump in. All of us was on the bed watching this debating over who was going to win. I would always choose Dad because I didn't like the fact that Mom always used weapons. My dad was about to jump in taking the risk of getting sliced just to beat up my mom. But before he got to her I stopped him in the process. I was too scared of what the outcome would be like. I was holding him back saying don't jump in, don't. Crying at the same time. Dad stopped, of course, and started to walk outside saying -Whoever wants to come with me come, and who ever wants to stay can stay. All of us wanted to go with my dad but my mom convinced my sister to stay with her. She did.

Months passed and our family managed to get back together. They would fight and make up. It wasn't no thing to me. We moved again down south in California. I remember living in a one-story house. At night when someone would wake up to go to the kitchen and turn on the lights we would see thousands and thousands of cockroaches running everywhere. We would get one slipper and try to stomp all of them while they was disappearing in the light. I was about five years old now, not going to school because of all the moving around we did. I don't remember living in a home for over six months. I remember moving more than anyone we knew. My dad said we basically lived everywhere in California.

Well, back about this house, it was a normal hot day like always. My mom took my little sister and went to the store while my dad, my brothers, and I were looking at clothes we had just gotten for free from a Salvation Army type of place. Hours past when my dad saw my mom coming in the house with my sister, he asked her -Where did you guys go? Mom responded that they went to the store. My dad then said - If you went to the store then where is the groceries? My little sister that went with her said innocently, "Hey, we didn't go to the store, we went to some guy's house." My dad got mad and mugged my mom saying cuss words. My mom got mad at my sister for telling on her and went to the kitchen and grabbed a knife to hit my sister with it. She didn't hit her with the sharp side, she hit her with the flat end so it wouldn't cut her, but Dad was not drinking so he just grabbed my sister and babied her saying that it is going to be all right.

When he doesn't drink he is the nicest person in the world. He doesn't care about material things. He chooses love over everything. I thought that since they didn't fight that it wasn't all that serious, but I knew my dad got heart broken because he couldn't do anything about the situation. If he was to beat her up then he would go to jail. He figured that if she is going to cheat on him she would do it no matter what cause my mom's side of the family is all fucked up. He hated her for doing that. He knew that she would just call the police if he beat her up. He really didn't want that to happen because then our family would be apart and his children without a father. There's a saying in our language that says: "A child without a father, is like a house without a roof." It is true to me. My father didn't like anything about my mom. After that, Dad took us to Washington to establish a new life.

On the freeway we go. Planing to stay with my uncle Cam Dang in Seattle WA. The only family we have in America. All I knew was Dad left everything behind him. He left behind our store we owned, one Teriyaki To Go and a seafood grocery store. He left the house, the car, his wife, and daughter. He basically left everything behind. He said that it didn't matter to him, that he would rather live without anything and a family that loves each other than a house with everything with no love. So we left. I don't know how my father managed to make it to Washington without speaking any English or anything. We was too small to even know the directions. The whole trip took like a couple of days. These days was the most fun days of my life. We stopped and took a look and checked out the scenery. I remember seeing two little tornadoes. We arrived in west Seattle at my uncle's apartment around 12:00am. The apartment complex was big. It seemed to spread around for about a mile or something. It was hard to find the apartment number. My dad tore us all a small piece of paper with my uncle's apartment number on it and told us to go and find the house, so we did. I went off on my own way and got lost. My brother had already found the apartment. I didn't know where everyone was so I started to cry. They ended up finding me, and I went inside and went straight to sleep. My dad and uncle was outside in the living room talking about grown-up stuff. What I find funny is that my grandfather back in Vietnam had named my dad Bia and my uncle Cam. In my language, Bia means beer and Cam means soft drink. My dad grew up to be an alcoholic and my uncle can't even drink one beer without getting fucked up. This was their conversation before I fell asleep.

We all woke up early in the morning. It felt crazy being away from Mom, sister, and California. The weather changed, everything changed, my life changed, and I needed to change also. I'd been wearing the same clothes for the longest. I had no clothes to change into. I wasn't going to school because I didn't have a steady home to stay in, and I couldn't make any friends.

We moved to a better area. I was about at the age of six now. One day walking home from school I remember a big girl was chasing me home and was beating me with a stick. I ran home crying and told everyone what happened, but everyone just laughed at me. My brothers at this time went to a school called the Wing Luk. I can remember coming home after school, and Dad would just beat the hell out of my brother Quy. He was suppose to write a letter for my dad because my dad did not know how to write in English, so my brother did. But he got beat up because the letter "c" looked like an "o." Now this wasn't just a regular beating. When my dad beat us up, he beat us up. He would consider us his enemy. He would give us his hardest punches and kicks. He also uses some kung fu on us. I didn't really think nothing of it, though. I was so used to the violence in our family, it was either mMom getting beat up or it was us. Dad use to just beat us up for no reason, he would just come up with something. Then he would put the blame on the alcohol. When he wasn't drinking he would often think about my mom and when he did, he would end up drinking, saying he drinks so he won't have to deal with the stress. But then when he does drink he thinks about my mom even more, then he would take it out on us by beating us.

I remember one day my dad caught my oldest brother Quy skipping school and found him sleeping in the closet. I can't even believe what he did to him. He beat the living shit out of him, I mean literally, he shit in his pants. The first thing he did was - he ran in the closet and kicked him in the face with his boots. My brother woke up immediately and screamed, crying, not expecting it. We lived in a two-story apartment. He was beating him hard on the top floor. The beating continued to the downstairs bathroom. When he got down to the bathroom he grabbed my brother's head by the hair and smashed it into the toilet. Then he dunked his head in the toilet water bringing him in and out of the water saying - Do you learn yet do you? My brother couldn't speak because of the water. I really didn't think that Dad was going to drown him so my other brother and I thought that he had deserved it. We was even telling Dad to go ahead and beat him up more and harder.

We stayed there for awhile but we ended up moving anyway. At this time Dad was working at a Chinese restaurant called the Wengs Garden. He would bring us home some guests' left over food because he didn't believe in throwing food away. He would come home in tears sometimes telling us how sad it was that Asian people throw away lots of good food in America and there is plenty of hungry people in our country. He was working as a dishwasher. I cry for him till this day. He bust his butt for us and we still made him mad. That is no job for an old man trying to raise four boys. He would walk miles and miles to go to work as a dishwasher. I can feel his pain. I know he cries at night thinking about his life, daughter, wife, and now his kids. He suffers for the love. My brother ended up finding a bike for my dad to ride to work. One day a neighbor kid went and told my dad that it was his bike so he just gave the kid his bike knowing that my brother had stolen it. He came home beating all of us and telling us to all lay down in a row of three and just whip and hit us for putting him in shame and stealing a bike. This was his way of disciplining us.

Ever since we moved up here from California I did not have a chance to meet or make any friends. We moved around too much. We ended up moving again, for what I do not know. We moved in with this one Vietnamese guy. He let us stay in his basement. It felt good for awhile just knowing that we lived in a house, even though it wasn't ours, and it was the basement. I got enrolled in School and had to walk for hours. This stupid girl that lived in our house also went to that school. She was either dropped off by her dad or she would take the school bus. Damn girl never asked me for a ride when she see me walking. Shit, she didn't even tell me where the school bus stop was. I think that she didn't tell me because she was ashamed to admit she knew me. I never had clean clothes to wear, I would wear the same clothes over and over again. I would still look cool because I knew how to do my hair. I would spray tons of hair spray and than make it stand up on the left side of my head like a fan.

My dad would do a lot of drugs and have a lot of parties. I could never get any sleep because it would be too loud. The only thing that separated the rooms was a blanket. I had to try and go to sleep with the smell of alcohol and weed smoke. One time there was this one white girl that my dad met and I was trying to go to sleep but I couldn't. I went out to the living room to tell my dad that it was too loud and smelly but he was just too high and drunk to care. He slapped me in front of all his friends and told me to shut up and go to sleep. I went in with my head down and started to cry. Hopped in bed with my brothers and tried to go to sleep. My brother Hoa was saying - It's going to be OK. Then out of nowhere I saw a lady come in the bed-room towards me. She came and picked me up and I guess felt sorry for me. She made my dad apologize to me and he did. I got all happy and kissed her and hugged her for a long time.

We moved again to a nicer neighborhood hoping to start all over because the owner of the house didn't like that my dad was having parties. I guess they couldn't get any sleep, either. Plus my brothers and I would sometimes get hungry, and we would sneak upstairs to try to cook some food in their kitchen. We didn't have a kitchen or a refrigerator downstairs. We would make bread with butter and mayonaise and put sugar on top of it. One time my oldest brother Quy got out of hand and took it too far. He went in the cupboards and cooked us some Kung Fu noodles. Then we would get caught, the family would yell at us, and when my dad got home, he beat us up. My dad was on welfare. I remember us always going to the food bank to get some food. Sometimes the food would be moldy. We would get our clothes from the Salvation Army pick-up area. Every Thursday we would go and pick up some furniture and clothes that people would donate to the Salvation Army. I barely went to school in clean clothes, but I made friends pretty well.

Now, my oldest brother Quy would get it the worst. Just because he is the biggest and the most wise one. Dad would make him take off all his clothes and put him in the garbage can outside in the snow. Things would get hectic to the point that he would often run away. Quy started living with my uncle Cam in west Seattle. He stayed there for about a year. Now, since he was gone, my dad used Hoa and me as a punching and kicking bag. I was too young to get beat up like an adult. I remember him tying my brother Hoa and I up and hanging us in the bedroom closet. Then he wouldn't feed us, threatening to burn us.

Out of my dad's sight and distance, Quy decided to join a gang called the O.F.B.z, known as the Oriental Fantasy Boys or the Original Fantasy Boys. His street name was PAUSE meaning staying still. His friends give him this name after a rumble with their enemy, a Samoan gang called the Mad Pac. When they were fighting, everyone in his gang was running around because the Samoans were much bigger than they were, but my brother didn't move so they called him PAUSE. I guess that's how he got his name. Then my uncle was tired of his friends and him being involved in the gangs so he decided to kick Quy out, and he came to live with us again.

During all this mess, my older brother Hoa and I was skipping school and getting into trouble, too. We went into major shoplifting because we saw everyone around us with nice things, and we wanted that stuff too. So, we went shop lifting because we never had any money. Our dad never bought us anything. Everyday we would go steal and just skip school for the fun of it and eat Asian noodles in the forest. I was about eight years-old with about a first grade education. I never had no toys so we would steal that too. One time we got caught and our dad beat us up bad, even though he was sober and he is never sober.

Now Quy was back in with us and Dad was happy. He admitted that even though he beat him up the worst that he loves us. He's just mad at the world and wanted to take out his anger on us. I guess he finds it very lonely to have one of his oldest sons not living with him. We are very close. All of us are close. We have a special bond that no one can understand. In our family, I grew up with nothing but guys. I never had a mom figure that really affected my life. So we basically did everything together. We took a shower together, eat and sleep and shit together. Ever since we moved to Seattle I slept with my dad and brothers.

Everything was going pretty good until one day, Dad got really drunk and fell asleep in the bedroom. He woke up around 7:00pm and went straight for the kitchen to get something to eat. Before he went to sleep he remembered putting two pieces of chicken in the rice maker, but when he woke up there was only one piece in there. He got mad at all of us and started to beat all of us for eating the piece of chicken, but no one ate it. I asked my brothers if they ate it, and they said -No, Dad is tripping. He ended up beating us pretty bad. My brother Quy figured that if all of us was getting beat up then he might as well take the blame and just get beat up by himself. Then my dad got even more mad saying - If you took the chicken then why did you let your brothers get beat up? He got beat up even worse. So basically he got the beating of his life for two pieces of chicken that never existed. He was so beat up that the neighbor saw the wounds and called the police. He told the neighbor and was like - No, don't call, if you do then he would beat us up even more. We told them that in our culture it is right for us to get beat up when we are wrong. I guess the white people did not understand that concept and called the police anyway. Then the police came and saw the wounds on him and took him in for questioning. He got tired of Dad beating him and decided that the white people's way was right. They even took me and Hoa in but when they would ask us about our wounds, we would just say that it came from each other and that we was just horse playing. We didn't want to tell on our dad. Not that we were afraid of him or anything, we just had too much love for him to see the police take him away.

My dad was put in jail for beating us up and drinking and driving. The time that Dad was gone I have to admit was the funnest time I had at this point and yet was the saddest. I missed dad being around, but on the other hand it was good because we didn't get no more beatings.

Quy was involved in gangs and always had friends over. I liked all of his friends, I thought that they were cool. Him coming from Seattle made all the neighborhood kids look up to him. He would often hang around the Heights Apartment known as the "ghetto" because of all the ethnic groups and the poverty households we was living in. It was mainly Asian kids. Everyone looked up to my brother because he would dress nice and have nice cars for his age, 16 or 17. So people wanted that lifestyle and decided to start their own little cliques doing criminal behavior activities. My brother Quy found a group of friends that he trusted and would hang around and have fun and just do the things that most teenagers do. But in this setting it was doing things that the average society would not accept because of his lack of parental guidance. My brother Hoa and I was just as bad. We started to go and rob little kids for their candy and money, breaking in houses, cars, steal and go beat up on the neighborhood white kids. It wasn't a bad thing to us. It was the only thing. One of my favorite things to do was to go and beat up on other people.

I was now about eight years old. I would go to school with a pocket knife. Because I remember my dad once told us we had to, just in case. There is a Vietnamese saying that goes big brothers and younger brothers don't be afraid of cowboys. They have guns, we have knives. If they pull the trigger, then we jump in and stab them.

One day the knife fell out of my pocket when I was out on recess. One of the teachers told me to go in the principal's office to talk about why I have a pocket knife. I responded that my dad is in the King County Jail and that I have no protection. The school then held a big meeting, and they were very supportive of me because I am from a one-parent house and the one parent that I have is locked up. I told them that my brother is only 14 years-old, and he is taking care of us. They then had a meeting. They decided to come up with this thing that would help us get food. They gave a donation box that had lots of food in it.

My dad, once in a while, would call and just say hi and see how we were doing. Then I would go hide in my room and just cry. My brother and I would take our anger out by going and fighting other kids. We would never lose a fight because we would be so used to the beatings. When you fight you don't get hurt as much as letting someone else hit and beat the hell out of you. That's why I am so used to getting black eyes and broken noses. I can take pain pretty good. I am used to the beatings. It made us tougher.

1992 started to get hectic for me. My father was back home. We were getting beatings again. My brother Hoa had just got arrested for sticking a knife to a kid's back and threatening that he was going to kill him. Me, I was just suspended for peeing in my teachers desk because I had to go to the bathroom. My older brother Quy was getting into bigger and better things. He even moved out and lived by himself. I guess he thought that he was getting too old for ass whippings. Him and his friends was on a mission wanting to go to Texas for a new lifestyle and go on a business trip. He went with three other friends that we call brothers. Their names I will not reveal because of respect. I will tell why later. But they were on their way. They were packed with lots of guns because they were robbing stores on their way to Texas. Before they got there they stopped in Arizona for a break from driving all that way. They pulled over to rest and sleep and out of nowhere a semi-truck ran them over killing two of them. My brother was put in the hospital with permanent brain damage. Dow was nearly dead, but the others were killed. In my culture, if someone dies you don't say their name, because you are letting them rest in peace. My brother Quy called my dad crying, saying that he is sorry and that he wants to come back home. This was a very important part in my life. My brother was only 18 and the other two were only 16 when they died. Rest in peace to my brothers. Quy was arrested after the accident, trying to escape from all the madness.

Hoa found himself with a group of gangs called the SAG, South Asian Gangsters. He started to not come home as much. Then when he did, Dad would beat him up. So he would get scared and not even want to come home for days. That kind of behavior led me to do that kind of stuff also. I started to not even come home for days, too. I never did understand my dad. I never did understand why he loves to drink so much. But now I can understand, his wife is gone, oldest son is gone, his younger sons are either gone or in jail, he doesn't even know where his daughter is or if she is even alive. And now I am running around and not coming home either. I know he cries at night. But he just doesn't show it. The reason he beats us up is because he just wants us to do good. He figures that he can drink and that will make him feel better. He really don't know how to be a father but he is mine. I wouldn't want no other.

Hoa was sentenced to two years and was sent to Green Hill school. Greenhill was for juvenile offenders. A mini prison like.

My dad was depressed even more now. It was to the point that he didn't care how we lived or even the conditions we was in. Me being who I am, I did care what I looked like and wanted to keep up with the trends - the nice Nikes and Dickies. I remember walking to a Place called King Center in Seattle, a big swap meet that sells homemade brand clothes. One time I got caught for stealing a pair of Dickies. The police took me to the precinct just to get my name down. He told me to give him a phone number so he can call my parents so they can come and pick me up. At this time in our home we didn't have any phone so I called my uncle to pick me up. Sometimes I would want to go to the detention because I felt that if I went there that I would have a better life.

I use to run away from home because I didn't like the conditions that I was living in. We wouldn't even have any food in our refrigerator. I would go to the Othello Safeway just to steal some food like bread and ham. It wasn't even my ethnic food but I managed to eat it. I can still remember one day my dad made me go to my neighbor's house to ask for some egg so we could cook it with some rice to eat and I did. All the money from our welfare, he should've used it for food, but instead he uses it all on drugs and alcohol. So I said to myself time and time again that there was no point to come home.

I remember taking the bus down to the Juvenile to see my brother. Those people would never let me in - they said that I needed an ID that proves that I was my brother's family. So I just went to the bus stop and took the bus to west Seattle and stayed at my friend's house until I could find a permanent place to live. Pretty soon all of my friends was getting tired of me, so I really had no place to stay. I was out on the streets. No one knew about it though. Everyday I would go to school like there was no problem. I was soon breaking into cars and stealing out of people's homes trying to find money. I even slept in cars when there was no place to go.

This went on for about five or six months, then I decided to try and go home. The next day I took the Metro bus to go home, and in downtown Seattle I got jumped by a whole bunch of Mexicans. I came home all bloody and sore, but Dad was too drunk to even notice. I walked in the house, and my dad just looked at me and he said to me, -What are you doing here? I looked at him in surprise and responded - I live here. Then he beat me up because I hadn't come home for a while. I ended up leaving again. This time I was gone for about a couple weeks. I ran out of places to stay. I took the bus back to my house, but when I got there my dad had already moved out that same night. I used the phone to call my brother Quy. I called him up and told him the situation. He decided to come and pick me up. He took me in, I was so happy. He lived in a nice apartment and all. Every day I would take the bus to school and back.

One day I invited a friend to come over and play with my brother's tattoo gun. I wanted to give one to him, but before I had a chance there was a knock at the front door. I didn't know that my brother had a contract with his parole officer that he couldn't be around gang members or else he would get put in jail for parole revoke. I opened the door, and it was some white guy. He asked me who I was, and I told him that I was Quy's brother and these are my friends. He looked at me and said OK and just left. When my brother came home I told him to call this guy on his card that he had given me, so my brother did. Couple hours later the police came and arrested my brother for breaking a parole violation. He was gone, so I had nowhere to go again.

I was back to sleeping in bus stops and at every house I knew. I even tried to go back to school. But I couldn't maintain. Because of all my moving I never got my homework done. I remember seeing my dad at the school. He asked me if I wanted to go and live with him at the new apartment. I came home for a couple of days and ran away again because he would always bring home some crack smoking friends. This is the last time I've seen him.

After the parole violation, Quy got out of jail and got a new apartment, and I ended up living with him again. He got me into this school where I was the only Asian kid that had gang life mentality. No one at the school liked me. The teacher always kicked me out of school and suspended me for some bullshit that a regular school would not do. My brother's girlfriend Nichole moved in with us at this point. I remember I never really liked her that much because I thought she was taking my brother's love away from me. At night I would steal her car and go kick it with my friends. She would call the police but they would never catch me. I got tired of taking her car, and I decided to go out and steal a car of my own. I would do this often, like once a week. I got caught a couple of times, but the system never really gave me much for it. They would always slap me in the hand which led me to keep on doing it over and over again. I learned how to steal cars from my brother. My favorite car to steal was the Honda Prelude. I once got caught with one in front of my friend's house when I was getting out of the vehicle. I did ten days in juvenile for it. The main reason I steal is because I would like to use the car for picking up girls and to be like my brothers.

Things started to get even better when my brother Hoa got out from serving a 2 and a half year sentence. I was about 13. We would go out and get drunk, high and just have fun. Go to clubs and start fights like old days when we was younger. We was wild. All the people that we knew, they know that we are crazy. Every time that they would have a party, and we would show up, they know that things are gonna get rowdy in there. It was to the point that we had a name for us it was called the BW and the PC. It stands for the Buck Wild and the Players' Crew.

One day my brother and I was getting drunk, and we just went outside and started to cry for no reason. We was talking about how fucked up our family was. Then we would talk about dad, and we would cry even more. We drove to Alki beach to just get away from everything. We decided to go and find our dad. No one had seen him for about two years. I called up my Asian counselor for help, and she said that our dad was in the hospital awhile back. So we went to the hospital and looked up his name. One of the nurse ladies told us that he was there for about a year because he was in a full body cast. I guess he was supposed to be paralyzed from the neck down. I was shocked. I couldn't believe that this would happen to my dad. They gave us this other place that they said he was at, and we went there to see. It was called the Mission. It was in some broken down building in downtown Seattle.

When I got there, it looked dirty and nasty. I saw a whole bunch of bums going in and out like I've never seen before. Out of nowhere I heard this voice like my father's voice. We hurried up the stairs where we heard the voice coming from. Out of nowhere I saw my dad. Now this is the saddest thing that I have ever seen in my life. I started to cry immediately. He was a bum, I told myself. In my head I couldn't believe this would happen to my dad. I never thought that Dad could be a bum. He was missing a tooth and he was all smelling like alcohol. He was dirty, and in his arms was a big bag of I don't know what. My brother and I went up to my dad and said in Vietnamese- Dad! Dad! He looked at us and kept on walking. He had a look on his face like these are just kids trying to rob him or start trouble or something. What made me sad was that he didn't even recognize us. Then he took a double-look and noticed that we was his kids. He looked at me and said my name twice- Tuan, Tuan? I looked at him and said- Yes, Dad, this is me. I start to cry, and he started to cry also. This is the saddest day in my life. There are no words in this world that can describe how I felt that day. It hurts to talk about it till this day.

He introduced us to his bum friends and was like bragging that we was his sons. My brother had brought his girlfriend with us, and my dad thought that she was his daughter. We took him to my brother Quy's house, and he was surprised. My brother and I was still crying. I still couldn't understand how he could be a bum. It hurts so much. I then told him to go wash up and get ready to eat. And he did. While he was in the shower I took a look in his bag. I found lots of things that made me even more sad. I found condoms, old sandwiches, cologne, razors, some dirty clothes, and some canned foods. I took it and put it away for him. I then went outside and cried again. He came out of the shower and my brother and I went and took Dad to the store, and we bought him some beer to drink. We drove to Alki beach and just drank and reminisced on the old days when we were all together. He sang us Vietnamese songs like he use to do when we was little in California. He started to cry and told us that he wasn't a good enough father which made me sad to hear. He told us why he became a bum. He tried to commit suicide thinking that he was at fault for everyone in our family being broken up. He then jumped out of a two-story building and landed on his feet. I feel it is my fault at times, that I should've stayed home instead of going out and not coming home. Only if I would of stayed home, I don't think that that would've happened. I just wanted to live the life in the fast lane, shit, I had no other choice. All I know was steal, rob, and basically the survival of the fittest. We ended up going home.

Out of nowhere we had a call from my little sister. She said that she wants to come home and live with us. I couldn't believe it. I hadn't seen her for over ten years. I remember my dad saying before he dies, he just wanted to see his daughter for one last time. It came true for him. For once in our life, we thought that our family had gotten back to one again. We came and picked her up at Seatac airport and ate in Seattle at a Vietnamese restaurant. Everything was back to normal. Our family is back again, and we cried. We cried happy tears.

But me being me, I was still stuck on that criminal lifestyle behavior. Not even two weeks later I committed a crime that caused me six years of life incarceration. For once in my life when I thought and felt my family has come to one, I went out to catch the bus to go to school. The bus never picked me up so I went and stole a car that had kids in it. It was out of innocence, because I was young. I didn't know what the consequences would be, thinking that it's just another t.m.v.w.o.p. and that I would get petty time for it. I've been slapped on my hand more than once for criminal behavior. That was just a tease for me. But this time since there was a baby involved, they charged me with kidnapping. I then immediately went on television nation-wide and was on the front page of newspapers. I thought that the whole thing was just out of hand. I figured that this wasn't that serious, that I have done many more things worse than this. At such a young age I already have a sentence that is over one third of my life.

I was sent to an institution that holds over three hundred male inmates. I spent the first couple years fighting and smoking and just doing everything illegal. To me, this place is like the capital of criminal education. I have seen people come and leave a better criminal. They call it rehabilitation. I say it doesn't rehabilitate you unless you are willing to be rehabilitated. How can you make someone normal, if he was never normal. What is normal? I had no other way to live than being in criminal behavior and having a criminal mind. I had no choice even if I wanted one. I figure - how are you going to tell a kid how to live when he has never seen that kind of life before? It's a struggle to know what is right and what is wrong when you live that lifestyle. Until you experience it you won't understand.

My first accomplishment was getting my high school diploma. This gave me the thought that I could do anything in life if I want it bad enough. I was the first one in my family that had ever graduated from high school. It's easy to say I could do anything. But I was once told that people may doubt what you say but will believe what you do. It is true. Now I'm at a point in my life that I understand everything in my life is a struggle. Being an Asian minority in a majority setting is even harder because I believe I, as a minority, will always, no matter how well I do, I will never be good enough. I've got to work twice as hard. I've got to fight any obstacle that heads my way and conquer it with ease, with time, through self-education, and having an open mind to reality. I was never taught that I had to be a certain race to be in power, but I found out the hard way. Sometimes it takes a little pain and struggle but the truth will reveal itself.

I never purposely used manipulation to get my way in an evil set of mind. I have to admit I have used it before, but not the way that it was taught to me by the system. I have learned how to use my head more wisely and chose my fights. Even though I can never win. I believe that there is no way to win if you are in a non-win environment. I just take in what I can and leave out what I can't take in. Through this time in here, (incarcerated), I've grown mentally and physically.

The main thing that has been keeping me on my toes this whole time is my brother Hoa. He is also locked up. He is in prison. He went in a little after I did. We have been writing back and forth supporting each other. It seems like he is the only one that understands me. It's probably true. I would just flash sometimes but thinking about him just makes me happy and have something to look forward to. I tell myself I will be out some day. I look at it like - for every dark night, there's a brighter day.

I would have to thank my experience of incarceration. I have taught myself many things, like truth and realism. I came to realize that you can't feel it until you have experienced the feeling. It's not just family, friends, and loved ones that you keep it real to or stay true to. It is mainly you. You are the only one who knows. I was once told "You've got to search deep in your heart to find what is fake and naturally you will be true." by HD (A.K.A. MD). Now I am who I am. A person of many opportunities. I am now attending Evergreen State College in Olympia Washington. I know where I'm from, who I am, and what I am capable of. But the most important thing in my life is what's the TRUTH !

With many more accomplishments to come.

As I sit here and relive my past, I gain a greater understanding of what incarceration has done to me. I come to feel a desire, no, a need to express my thoughts, experience my pain and suffering that was and still is inside me. My goal is to prove to those in my situation or worse that there is a brighter day for every dark night. I hope to let them know that they are not alone and that they too can find a way back home. Whether it's freedom, religion, family, or keeping your sanity, you can be a somebody, a special person to this world.

When you think everything is going your way and that you can close a chapter in your life, before you know it, another one opens. With my experiences of living life, love and truth is what it boils down to. With love, whether it is for people or material things, it involves others. The truth is, someone's gonna get hurt. Live for yourself because no one will live for you. With the power of love, people may say at times, "I will die for you." They probably would, but ask yourself, is the love for them stronger than the love you have for yourself? There is no right or wrong when it comes to love. Shit, when it comes to life, period. Follow your heart, do what is best, and if it is not recognized as "right" then who is wrong?

Change, people change. For the better, hopefully not for the worse. Who decides whether your change is wrong or right.

You and only you can judge yourself. People may hear what you did but will not see what you will do because a head is a mind of judgment. Everyone does it. Especially people with artificial power (people who believe in oppression, they lack control in their lives so they control others). These people believe in the root of all evil (money). Money has power to say what is wrong or right. So those people judge. Those people need to change their thoughts and ways of thinking.

Before judging the one that has no choice but live the way he does remember if we the people could choose our lifestyles at our adolescence to live a "perfect American dream," do you think we would grow up to be judged?

Tuan Ngoc Dang

MY STORY

BEN PETERS

*I am a Native American. I don't say
Indian because we are not from
India. The white people called us a
false name which people fail to
realize. We are not from India. We
are from here on Turtle Island, or as
some call it, the United States.*

My name is Benjamin Alfonso Peters. But I go by the name Ben. I'm eighteen years old. Right now I'm currently doing some time here at "Maple Lane School," a juvenile institution in Washington state for youth who committed crimes. I'm writing this autobiography for myself and to share my life's experience to those who may be interested. It may not be the best writing or grammar or even the best life. That's not my concern. So if you don't appreciate my time and effort I put into my story, oh well. I'm still movin on. I hope you can implement something from my life to yours.

I was born on November 13th, 1981 in Olympia, Washington to my mother Gale Longshore and my father Edwin Peters. I am a Native American. I don't say Indian because we are not from India. The white people called us a false name which people fail to realize. We are not from India. We are from here on Turtle Island, or as some call it, the United States.

My dad was probably ninety percent Native American with a little bit of Mexican. I can't confirm the Mexican part for sure, though. My mom was a little over half Native American, which makes me basically seventy percent Native American and Mexican and Irish.

I'm enrolled in the Skokomish Tribe of Tawana from Washington. My father was from a tribe called Wailacki in Mendocino County, northern California. My mom and dad divorced when I was around four years old. I have slight memories of when I was a baby. I still have memories of when me and my parents lived in Tumwater, Washington. I lived an all right childhood raised by single parents.

I have two half brothers. Leslie Lewis Lincoln is now twenty-four years old. That's my mom's son. My brother, Lamar Peters, is my oldest half brother. He is my dad's son. I don't know my oldest brother very well. I've seen him rarely in my lifetime. However, I do accept him and his kids, my nieces and nephews.

When I was four years old or so, my parents moved to the Skokomish reservation where my mom's people are from, just north of Shelton. When my mom and dad were together, there was a lot of domestic violence. My dad used to beat my mom, mostly when he was drunk. He would treat my brother disrespectfully because he wasn't his son. My dad never put his hands on me. And I have not the slightest clue why. Perhaps because he loved me more than anything else.

That's when my mom and dad divorced. My dad moved back to his home in California, to the Round Valley Indian Reservation where he and his people are from. I have foggy memories of when I went to California with my dad. I was young. I graduated out of Head Start. My dad treated me well and took me everywhere with him no matter what.

I hardly ever had any babysitters. My dad was an alcoholic. He used to drink all the time. So did my mom, but not as much because she worked for the Skokomish Tribe for years.

I returned to Washington two years later from California to finish kindergarten and the first grade. That was at Hood Canal School. I was at Hood Canal until someone tried to burn down the school. So while the school was getting rebuilt, I went to finish my first grade year at Wyhelute school in Nisqually, Washington. I barely remember that school. I know that some of my cousins went there with me, so I wasn't alone. When the Hood Canal School got fixed up, I went there to do the second grade which I completed with no problems.

I went back down to California to stay with my dad. I was doing my third and fourth grade which was all right. I liked taking turns staying with my parents and being with both sides of the family.

Everything was going good for me in California. I went to a few pow wows and played in little league baseball. I played for the Coyotes as a left fielder. Things was going good in my life. Until one day at one of my baseball games, my dad was drunk and one of his buddies let him borrow his truck. My friend and I got in the back and we took off. My dad was driving really fast and tried to drive through a creek bed, where the road crosses the creek, and we wrecked into the bank of the road.

I got knocked out or something. All I know is I woke up bawlin my eyes out and had a big cut in my head. I had to go to the hospital and get thirteen stitches in my head. As soon as my mom found out about the accident, she drove down to California and picked me up and back to Washington we went.

The travelling back and forth started getting to me. But my parents couldn't live together so that's the way it had to be.

When I came back up to Washington, everybody looked different. All my friends and family grew older. Back to Hood Canal school I went for my fifth grade year. I got pretty good grades in school, only because my dad used to make me bring home homework, especially when I was in the fourth grade. I used to play the violin, and boy, my dad used to make me practice. And I got better. I even played at a Christmas concert held at the Round Valley Elementary School. But I never did want to play another instrument again. I just wasn't interested anymore.

When I was in the fifth grade at Hood Canal School, I graduated from the D.A.R.E. program they had there. And I remember making many promises to my mom that I'd never do drugs. But that promise was meant to be broken. Because when the fifth grade was over, I was on my way back to California. A little older and a little more curious.

That summer, I think it was 1993 or so, I started smoking cigarettes at eleven years old, thinkin I was cool. Then I started smokin marijuana and then to drinkin. Basically one thing led to another. I didn't drink that much because I didn't like it. But I did love smokin marijuana. That became an every day thing. My father said he minded, so I smoked marijuana even more.

Around this time my grandma Eva was getting old and sick. So most of the family spent a lot of time with her.

In California during my sixth grade school year I did really bad in school. I went from fighting to smokin marijuana in the bathroom to just getting kicked out of school. Then I just said screw it and quit school.

I only went to school every other day. My dad didn't care because the teachers were racist against Native Americans. My cousins were getting involved in gangs and since I was around them all the time I dressed like them and acted like them. My cousins were from the "Nortenos." I never got courted into their gang but was still down with them and liked their style. My dad still didn't care what I was getting involved in.

To me, my dad was cool. He always gave me money and did things for me in the best way he could. My mom and dad were two different parents. So I got used to my dad's rules because they seemed better than my mom's.

I always use to see my cousins in Ukiah, a small city in California, and visit them. It was fun until the summer came. My grama Eva was dying, and then one day, she was on her death bed at home. Everybody was visiting my Grandmother. One day she closed her eyes and didn't wake up. It was sad for me because I loved my grandma. We had a big funeral. My grandma had a lot of kids, grandkids, and even great grandkids. She passed away in 1994.

My dad was dealing with his grief in his own way, along with everybody else. But my dad dealt with his grief by drinkin, and I was still livin life the way I lived it. A month or so later my dad and I went to Ukiah to see my cousins again. I was around twelve years old. My dad dropped me off with my cousins and left. That was the last time I saw him.

One day or so later at night, my uncle Leonard came in my cousins' house cryin, saying he was so sorry and hugged me really tight. I was a bit confused because I was on speed. Then he told me my dad was dead. That he got stung by bees.

I went to see my dad in the hospital. His body was really swollen and pale. My dad was really allergic to bees. I started to cry because I felt if I had been there that shit wouldn't have happened. I cried hard that night. My dad passed away August 4, 1994, about a month after my grandma Eva died. That was the drastic part, I thought. But there is still more death to come.

Now my family was busy arranging my dad's funeral. My mom heard about my dad's death and as usual came down to California to get me. My mom also went to my dad's funeral.

My mom and I were on our way back up to Washington. Me, a boy with no father. I felt sad because I knew my life was gonna change in a whole nother way, and it did. When I came back up to Washington I didn't act the same. I couldn't, or should I say wouldn't, follow my mom's rules. I got too used to my dad's rules. I felt angry inside because my mom had her boyfriend and I wasn't tryin to have no father. I had only had one father and he was dead. There ain't no one who could replace him.

So I went to seventh grade at Hood Canal School and did alright for a while. I started skippin school left and right. I constantly didn't listen to my mom. So she turned me over to C.P.S. I had to go to this group home in Olympia called Haven House for ten weeks.

I ran away from Haven House but came back a day later. I then went to a foster home in an all white people family. I had four foster sisters. That foster home was an interesting place. I went back home sixteen days later.

Me and my mom got along much better. I went on a field trip to South Dakota when I was around thirteen years old. I seen the Bad Lands and Mt. Rushmore, which wasn't too exciting. I went back to Hood Canal School for the eighth grade but still had problems in school. Whenever I got in any kind of trouble at school, I would just walk home. I remember around that time my mom got a phone call. The message was my uncle Leonard Peters got shot to death by the police. He was the father of the cousins I mentioned earlier.

So me and my mom packed up some stuff and headed for California for my uncle's funeral. That's my third funeral in two years. I lost another family member. I really started feeling like my dad's side of the family was going down. Because before that, my uncle Arylis murdered somebody and got sentenced to 35 to Life in Pelican Bay State Prison. I basically lost him, too.

Anyway, my mom and I came back up to Washington. I wanted to stay in California really bad. I didn't finish my freshman year of high school. As a matter of fact, I didn't even finish the eighth grade. The school just passed me.

During that time as a freshman I was pretty much doing my own thing. I use to sell marijuana and stay at my house most of the time. I got pulled out of high school and went to a treatment center in Spokane, Washington called the Healing Lodge of Seven Nations. I was only there two days before I ran away. I was runnin around in Spokane, Washington. I didn't know where to go so I came back to the treatment center. I went home eight days later.

I remember how I use to babysit my niece Kierah. That's my brother Leslie's daughter. I love that kid. She's my favorite person. I liked babysitting her, since my brother was always too quick to give her away to a babysitter. My mom and I would always be glad to take her.

I tried speed again and kinda liked it. I wanted more so I stole a purse out of a car for money, but there was none in there. I broke into one of my old friend's brother's trailer and stole a Russian s.k.s. rifle. Somehow the cops found out and were after me and my friend.

The cops found me and my friend at another friend's house. They had the house surrounded. My friend and I decided to make a run for it. We ran out the back door and they caught my friend because he fell down. I kept on running and didn't get caught.

While the cops took my friend to jail, I was on the loose. I started to regret what I did. I thought that what I did was stupid. I only did it because I needed money. Now there was no turning back. I thought retribution must be done.

One night I seen all the Skokomish tribal police in their building. This crooked idea popped into my head. So I went and siphoned some gas. Then I went back to the building and began dumping gas on all the exits and around the windows. It was pouring down raining. I went to light the building. My lighter wouldn't light because I was soakin wet, along with the lighter. Before I knew it, there was a cop outside standin there lookin at me. I threw the gas can and ran.

My body was burned because I spilt gasoline on myself. So I went home to take a shower and change my clothes.

That didn't work out. When I got dressed, I went to go out the front door and there was about ten cops surrounding my house. I was booked.

I went to Mason County jail, got fingerprinted then went to juvy in Thurston County for one day. The next day I went to Grays Harbor juvy. I was locked up for my first time. I committed my first offense. I sat at Grays Harbor for four months waiting trial.

I was lookin at five to fifteen years. The courts, I think, were tryin to scare me. I wasn't scared though. My mom was scared.

I didn't really have no case because I had a pretty bad lawyer and couldn't afford my own. I pleaded guilty to all charges. I got charged for third degree theft, third degree burglary, and first degree attempted arson. I got sentenced to 149 to 204 weeks. I wasn't going home for awhile.

I got sent up to Maple Lane School on May 23rd, 1997. This was my new home for a while. During my first eighteen months in Maple Lane, I was getting in trouble left and right. I started to get my act together and got an interview to go to Mission Creek, a youth camp in Belfail, Washington.

I went to Mission Creek. I was only there seventy days, then escaped one night. It sucked being on the run, but it also felt so good to be free again. I already had been locked up almost two years at the time. I was on escape for only nine days and got turned in by my mom. I didn't know she was the one who turned me in until later.

I went to Mason County Juvenile for a day then got sent to Green Hill School for a few days. Green Hill is another Juvenile Institution for youth who commit crimes. I got sent back to Maple Lane three days later.

I was back at Maple Lane for about a week and had a visit by my mom. A few days later I got a call from my brother that my mom was in the hospital with a five percent chance to live.

I went to the hospital that night to see my mom laying there unconscious. I said my good-byes. The next day she passed away. I took it hard, but not as hard as everybody thought. My mom died on

May 2nd, 1999. I went to my mom's funeral and said good-bye for the last time. I seen most of my friends and family there and seen my mom get buried. Even some of my aunts came up from California to support me.

I went back to Maple Lane, doing my time, feeling alone. I lost my grandma, two uncles, my father and my mother. Could things get any worse?

I went back to the population and got my G.E.D. I learned how to "fancy dance," that is a certain Native American styled dance for pow wows. The Native Americans had their own pow wow at Maple Lane. I went to sweat lodge ceremonies since I've been at Maple Lane. I started learning more about my tribe and my culture by reading books. My tribe is Skokomish, so I studied the Tawana culture.

I started attending weekly college classes with the Evergreen State College. I got four credits going on eight. I'm tryin to learn my language, the Tawana language. It's hard to do by myself because I need a teacher to help interpret for me. I'm also studying and learning about my dad's tribe in California, the Wailacki.

I've been locked up thirty-nine months now. I've been through a lot since being locked up. I smoked marijuana, cigarettes and made alcohol. I've been in fights. I've gotten jumped. I've gotten things stolen from me. I've stolen from others. I've experienced a lot of manipulation from the employees who work in this institution and residents. Right now I'm in drug and alcohol treatment. If I complete it, that's my first step in going home earlier than my maximum release date.

One main thing I learned since I've been incarcerated is knowing who your real friends are. Not many friends write or call you here. I am not worried about that, I'm just tryin to get out earlier than my maximum release. My minimum release is already past due to my past anti-social behavior. I got a little bit of time left in the in-patient treatment program.

I'm hopefully gonna go home soon. I'm not lookin back when I leave these gates. I have some goals and one is to go to college. The other is to learn my native language with an elder from my tribe. I don't plan on committing any more crimes and getting locked up again. That would be pure ignorance on my part. I can't afford to lose any more than I already lost.

I'm not sure what I wanna be. I'm still young and hopefully will think of something soon. For now I just wanna learn about my tribe's culture from both sides of the family.

This is eighteen years of my life, my experiences that I am willing to share with you, with more to come. Hopefully next time I will be old with a lot of kids. I gotta keep my name going.

Thank you for taking your time to read my story. I hope you learned something and got something out of it.

TANGLED UP
VIGOROUS CYCLES OF LIFE

SIMEON TERRY

*In truth, life may more than once call upon you
to prove who you are by demonstrating an
aspect of who you are not, and that's the way I
look at my adolescent years, as a time of growth
in the mind. As frustrating as it may have been,
it was a transformation in the making of an
entirely different person.*

I stood in the hallway of the house where I lived. My dad came down the stairs and stopped at the front door. I walked over to him slowly, and he said something about leaving. He opened the door. I remember asking him where he was going, but I don't remember him saying anything. I just remember standing in the doorway looking at his back as he proceeded down the second flight of steps in front of our house. That would be the last of my experience with a two-parent family, although at the time I had no idea what a two-parent family was because I myself was only two years-old.

I didn't even understand the extent of what had just happened and yet this was the first memory of my life. Not a very good memory to grow up on for a young child or for anyone, but it's been an all-too-familiar trend in the US during the 80's and 90's. I don't know the exact statistics, but I'm sure a majority of incarcerated youth grew up in a single parent family. I'm not saying that because one parent decides to split from the family that that's the whole reason a child would stray off from community standards and commit crimes thus becoming incarcerated like myself. I'm saying that with all that happens in a child's adolescent years, growing up in an environment with only one superior, one person to help you, one adult to keep an eye on you, and one parent to teach you the necessities of life that it's just another factor (and a big one at that) that adds on to the hardships of life. It's simple; two is better than one in almost any case and the times that my mom couldn't spend with me, maybe my dad could have, making my life a little more structured instead of going out and experiencing things on my own, ultimately "doing it the hard way" almost every time. But you must also trust the impeccable flow of life. Its symmetrical system is flawless in every way. It cannot not be perfect in all its magnificence. The tapestry of its design is pure perfection. You cannot cheat life nor can life cheat you. Therefore, the path that you choose will propel you through life towards the destination of liberation or enlightenment, which is the destination of every chosen and unchosen path possibly and impossibly conceivable to the human mind.

Survival comes first in every aspect, and this my mom provided for my sister and me from the day we were born. One parent can teach their child many things, but it's pretty damn hard to teach them everything they wanna know because they won't always say, "hey, mom/dad, what's it feel like to have sex or to experience drugs and alcohol?" Odds are, when there's only one parent, the child's a lot more likely to go find out about certain things on his/her own. So in my life, growing up without a father figure turned out to be a high potency chemical, that if mixed with the 'wrong' components would cause turmoil and upheaval in the already flawed foundation of the family. My future years of growing up proved to supply ample ingredients for such chaos.

Growing up in my younger years, it seemed, was pretty "normal." I had plenty normal. I had plenty of friends and always had something fun to do. The red flags in my childhood weren't too noticeable unless you really looked for them, so that's what I did, I looked for them. And by doing this, I constructed an outline of my life using a sort of stepping stone method that was taught to me by a wonderful woman by the name of Marilyn Frasca, a now retired writing instructor. So by using this method, I am hoping to bring forward at least one significant experience each year of my life. But before I go on to the next story, let me introduce myself with a brief description.

My name is Simeon Daniel Terry. I know it doesn't have a nice ring to it like some names but it's better than what my dad first came up with - St. Michael Xavior the 3rd.

"Mark, there has to be a first and a second before there can be a third," my mom explained. "No there doesn't," my dad replied, but decided to go with Simeon after taking a time-out in the corner and thinking about what he had just said.

I was born in Spokane, WA on May 12, 1980, a day after Mother's Day and six days before Mt. St. Helen's erupted. I was raised in Spokane for most of my life. It's a pretty decent city to grow up in, but not very multicultural. I myself am mulatto so most of my friends were of various ethnicities. I had plenty of white friends, probably more than most biracial kids. I had a sort of natural gift to get along with everybody and I still do, although it's somewhat harder to demonstrate while I'm incarcerated.

Some people think they gain by taking your kindness for weakness, so it can sometimes be difficult to be kind, if that makes any sense. For the most part I try to treat everyone equally and with respect even if they've done something against me, because karma is around every corner. You can't avoid the same energy that you send out, but you can choose what kind of energy it is that you use. I didn't always live this truth though. It took a lot of physical time and experience to decode my true self and to decipher who I really am. My child's mind knew who I was but my adolescent era started questioning my self as a person, which in turn was good because it meant I had a mind of my own. In truth, life may more than once call upon you to prove who you are by demonstrating an aspect of who you are not, and that's the way I look at my adolescent years, as a time of growth in the mind. As frustrating as it may have been it was a transformation in the making of an entirely different person.

Some people are just born with "rebel without a cause blood," and I was one of them. The first rebellious act I can remember was when I was three years-old. It was sunny outside, and I believe it was a Saturday because my mom always made something good for breakfast on the weekends. We were regular church goers, so I'm pretty sure it wasn't Sunday, but I could be wrong because there was a maintenance man working on our house.

I was in the front yard playing with the neighbor girl Rachae, who was the same age as me. The maintenance man had a ladder posted on the side of the house that reached to the part of the roof where there was a little flat area where people could stand and walk around on. I was watching him with my three year-old fascination. It looked like he was fixing the gutter or something. My mom came out on the front porch and asked the man a couple questions. The man came down the ladder and joined my mom on the porch to answer her questions. My mom then invited him inside, but before they entered the house, I distinctly remember my mom saying, "Now, Simeon, don't go messing with so and so's ladder or tools." For some reason, I don't recall what my response was. I just remember persuading Rachae to follow me up the ladder and onto the roof where we sat down and started having a normal three-year-old conversation. I was enjoying myself until my mom came out onto the front porch calling my name. I listened to her a couple times before shouting back, "What!"

She said, "Your pancakes are ready."

"OK, I'm coming," I yelled back.

It must have sounded odd to my mom that my voice was coming from directly above her so she asked, "Where are you?"

My response was, "Right here."

My mom again asked, "Where?"

I simply responded, "On top of the roof."

The tone of my mom's voice rapidly changed from that of a confused and wondering voice into a now ferocious rage of utter displeasure. "Get your tail down from there this instant, young man," my mom screamed out.

"I'm coming," I said, making my way down the ladder, getting a tongue lashing even before I touched ground.

"Is Rachae up there too?" my mom implied.

"Yeah," I said looking at my feet in a shameful posture.

"Rachae, you come down here right now, you're in big trouble too," yelled my mom.

Rachae poked her face over the side shaking her head no. I don't know if she was afraid of getting in trouble by her mom or if she was just too scared to go back down the ladder. My mom tried to coax her down for a minute or two until the maintenance man said he'd just go up and bring her down himself. So he did, while tears rolled down her face with every step Mr. Maintenance took. My mom continued to yell at us, stressing the fact of how we could have fell off and hurt ourselves.

I didn't intentionally do it to disobey my mom or to make her angry. I just thought it would be funny to trick her, by making her wonder where I was at. The problem was that I didn't really think in full what the outcome of the situation would be. I know I was extremely young, but I can remember this like it was yesterday, literally. I remember using my brain like any person would do no matter what the age. Not thinking ahead is common with kids, but as time goes on it usually gets better, you pretty much learn your lesson and think of punishment and consequences before you think about doing something that you know you shouldn't do. But for me, I had another way of thinking. I just told myself that I wouldn't get caught no matter what I did. And because of that, I just stopped thinking about consequences all together which in turn caused my rebel acts to increase as I grew older. In this case, I knew my mom would find me on the roof, but I didn't know she would be that mad because this was my first time acting against my mother or anybody that I can remember. I wasn't even trying not to get caught, I don't even think my mind comprehended something like that at that age, but I caught on early.

A year later I was with my babysitter at a local grocery store and as we were walking by the candy section I saw something that I wanted. We stopped right where the gum section was so my babysitter could look at a magazine. I remember seeing a commercial of Bubble Yum on TV a couple of days earlier so I really wanted the gum but I knew my babysitter wouldn't buy any for me. I quickly grabbed a pack and put it in the front right pocket of my pants while no one was looking. After we left the store I thought to myself, 'that's easy, I should just do this every time I want something that I can't usually have.'

When we got back to my babysitter's house I went outside in the front yard to play with some of the neighbor kids. I was giving some gum to another kid when, Marsha, my babysitter abruptly came out of the front door and specifically asked, "Where'd you get that gum from, Simeon?"

I replied with a simple, "I found it." I don't remember much after that, but she probably said something like "Where did you find it?" and I probably said something like, "I don't remember." I had two great lines as a kid that adults couldn't really decide if you were lying or not. I'm sure they thought you were, but they couldn't prove it, they couldn't really put their finger on it. The first one was, "I found it." And the second one was, "My mom said I could." If I had just stole something and somebody asked me where I got it I would say "I found it" every time. Me and my best friend even stole a dog and told his mom we found it. I think we even took his collar off so it would look like he was a real stray.

My first little act of violence involved a dog, too. It was a different dog, but it was with the same best friend, Chris. Chris was biracial like myself. Half-Mexican, half-white, but he looked full white. Whenever I would go out somewhere with him and his mom, people would think she was my mom and he was just my friend. My mom was full white so whenever Chris went somewhere with us it was vice versa. Chris was somewhat demanding as a best friend and slightly more devious, although I threw in my fair share of rotten behavior. Together as a team we raised havoc in the neighborhood, terrorizing kids, grown-up neighbors, pedestrians walking along, and cars that frequently drove by. And we weren't very friendly to my mom's boyfriend's dog named Cujo. It wasn't as crazy as the dog in the movie, but it was still pretty wild.

Well, one day myself, Chris, and my sister were in my front yard eating some sandwiches for lunch when Cujo came out from somewhere. He was sniffing at our food and trying to eat it out of our hands. Cujo decided he wasn't going for that and started jumping up on us, making us fall down, dropping our food on the ground and quickly eating it up before we knew what happened. Little did Cujo know, me and Chris weren't going for it either.

We calmed him down and led him through the next door neighbor's yard and over to Chris's house. We proceeded to coax Cujo up the stairs and onto the balcony. We both grabbed a pair of legs and lifted him over the rail. We let him go. That is, we let go of his legs and dropped him. He hit the ground with a loud yelp and just stayed there, crouched down, for a couple hours. We thought that would teach him a lesson and I guess it did because I don't remember any further attacks.

I always liked guns as a kid. Even though my mom never bought me toy guns or even allowed them in the house I still managed to always be around them. My mom said I'd find sticks that resembled guns, make guns out of my legos, and even chew my toast into the shape of a gun. I spent most of my childhood free time playing World War III with Chris and other neighborhood kids since he had an abnormal supply of toy guns. There's a lot of other things I did to my neighborhood that I won't mention, a lot of destructive behavior. Just know I caused plenty of havoc in the 'hood. I remember tripping a boy at school who I didn't like and kicking dirt in his face like "Roadblock" did on a GI Joe cartoon I saw. I don't know if it was TV that provoked me, but it probably had something to do with my attraction to violence. But karma doesn't forget and a while later it came back and got me.

When I turned seven, my mom got me a bike for my birthday. I already knew how to ride a bike so I was out riding around all the time. I soon learned that all the older "cool" kids had their seats up high so of course I wanted to raise mine as well. The only problem was, I never liked to ask for help on anything. I didn't even like people knowing what I was doing, I don't know why. I guess it's in my genes, because my dad's the same way.

So I got some wrenches and screwdrivers without my mom knowing and went to work on my bike. I didn't know all you had to do was loosen the seat pole and raise it up. I thought it had something to do with the seat itself so I started unscrewing all the bolts and screws underneath the seat. Well, the seat came off and over a dozen metal pieces were laying on the ground. I didn't know what I'd done or how to put it back together so I got mad and just threw all the pieces in the garbage. I went and told my mom, but she said she didn't know how to fix it and that I just had to ride it without a seat. I was thoroughly disgusted and just left my bike in the backyard to get rained on.

After a couple of days my mom said Randy, her boyfriend, had a surprise for me out back in the alley. Yep, you guessed it. It turned out Randy had gotten all the pieces out of the garbage and put everything back together and even raised my seat for me. I was so happy I jumped on my bike and sped off down the street as fast as I could. About half a block from a busy intersection I stopped pedaling and just coasted. When I tried to press on the brakes I couldn't because the pedals were spinning around and I couldn't reach them that good while I was sitting on the higher seat. I didn't want to jump off because I was wearing shorts and no shoes so I ended up coasting right out into the path of oncoming traffic. Boom!! A car hit me on my left side and I flew into its windshield. The car then slammed on the brakes (which you shouldn't do) and I flew off the hood, did a couple barrel rolls and came to a stop about 10 feet in front of the car, while the driver immediately started shouting, "I didn't see him, he came out of nowhere," and things to that effect. I got up in seconds and walked to my bike unfazed. I was just thinking "Whoops, just got hit by a car, better go home and tell Mom." But I didn't make it that far, people just started coming out of the woodwork and trying to restrain me. They made me lay down and told me to be calm, that I needed an ambulance and one was on the way. So I did what they said because adults were always right.

My sister Lisette had seen what happened and raced home on her Big Wheels to tell my mom who was stacking wood on our front porch. My mom almost tripped and fell, she jumped off the porch so fast. She made it to the scene, about 2 blocks away, in less than a minute. The ambulance got there shortly after and took me to the hospital. It turned out that I only needed a band-aid for my left knee which had a cut on it, but still costing my mom over $200.00. She was kind of mad, but I tried to tell her that it wasn't my fault, that if those people hadn't restrained me and called 911 then I could have just went home and got a band-aid for free.

After that I decided not to trust adults that much. I thought they had tricked me on purpose so I decided I wasn't going to fall for any more deceptions again. In fact, I planned to start going against them. The next summer Chris and I went on an all day bicycle trek from store to store. It all started when we went to a little store called the White Elephant which had pretty much everything from little kids' toys to handguns and assault rifles. We went in there and stole about eight knives from the front counter. We acted like our dad was around the aisle and walked to the back where we were out of sight and put the merchandise in our pockets. Chris even managed to put a machete down his pants and get away in a close call. We thought it was pretty funny and exciting so we continued to do it all day and the next day and the next day. We were too young to look like a threat to any of the store clerks. The only time we were really watched was when we went into the little convenience stores like 7-11 and Exxon, but we were still never caught or even questioned. We didn't want to be caught or questioned by our parents either, so we put everything we stole in my tree house except for our knives, which we kept at each other's house.

Most kids that were my age had a collection of baseball cards or stamps or something. I had a collection of cromies and all kinds of knives. I don't know why I had to be different, but it was little differences like that, that led to my explosive teenage behavior.

The next summer, when I was nine, I got into a little trouble with the police. When I was a little younger, one of my mom's boyfriends told me that jail was a dungeon that had flesh-eating rats in it that would slowly eat you alive starting with your toes, and boy, was I glad to have escaped that. Getting thrown in the back of a police car at age nine for messing with some guy's house had me on spook status for a while but there was still a problem. I knew it was a close call, but I thought I had gotten away without being caught. I wasn't in jail so I wasn't caught, that's how I rationalized it. After I regained composure and got a little dare back in my gut I continued going to stores and stealing while still looking innocent from my young childhood appearance. But the next year I got caught again and basically the same thing happened.

I was at a no-name gas station on my side of the tracks, which is pretty much the "ghetto," where everybody looks at everybody else with suspicious eyes because the crime rate is so high. They didn't nickname the area "felony flats" for nothing. So I was inside the gas station taking my time putting things in my pocket. I was sure they hadn't seen me do anything so I attempted to buy some candy as well. I put a quarter on the counter and said, "I'll take this."

They looked at me as if I was a complete moron and asked, "This is all you're going to buy after being in here for 20 minutes?"

I said, "Yeah," and they asked what I had in my pockets.

I pulled my jean pockets out and said, "nothing."

They pointed to my coat and said, "Empty'em now."

I pulled out a handful of merchandise and responded with a quick lie stating, "Oh, these, I bought these here yesterday."

The lady talking to me replied with a calm, "Why don't you step behind the counter so we can let the police take care of this." At the mention of the police I bolted for the door, but was blocked off by a big fat biker lookin' dude. He grabbed me by the arm and escorted me back behind the counter where I had to sit on a milk crate while I waited for the police to come pick me up.

A police officer came and got me, put me in the back with handcuffs on and took me home only because I pleaded and convinced him

I'd never do it again. My mom was extremely mad this time and gave me severe consequences, but I still felt I had gotten off and escaped real punishment. Not only did I think that not going to jail meant not being caught, but I had thought back on the crime and figured out what I done wrong. I wasn't thinking the crime itself was wrong though, I was analyzing the situation and brainstorming a better way to commit crimes of this nature in the future. I think if I had been put in the juvenile at that young age I would have chilled out and stopped acting a fool. Or maybe if I had a father figure, I would have been too scared to get in trouble for fear of physical discipline. I know I can't change my past or predict what would've happened, but the future of others can be shaped to fit the kind of life that will perfectly serve them. Little did I know I was caught in between two worlds and I was crossing over on the wrong bridge, a bridge that would be sure to self-destruct in a hazy future.

At the age of 11, I became more destructive, leaving a backyard full of wreckage. I took every toy I owned and smashed them with an old rusty hammer I had found in the bushes. I got every toy I could find and put them on an old cutting board and smashed them into oblivion one at a time, discarding the pieces into a pile under my tree house. I then destroyed my tree house as well, throwing the debris every which way around the yard. The door to my garage was swinging back and forth in the breeze, each time hitting the side of the garage. The sound was beginning to annoy me so I punched and kicked numerous holes in the door rendering it useless for its purpose. The only thing really left standing in my yard besides the barbecue was the swing set that my sister and I had played on just years earlier.

Although the sky was clear and somewhat sunny, my mind was filled with black clouds and a thunderous forecast. I saw an old wooden bat laying in the dirt and proceeded to pick it up, not knowing I was in the midst of buying a one way bumpy ride to sin city, and I'm not talking about Las Vegas. I hit the swing set repeatedly until it was mangled and gnarled into a horrific scene of art. I was satisfied with what I had done and went back inside to wait for my mom to come home from church. She was pretty disgusted with me about the garage door but didn't seem to care about the other stuff, just kinda wondered why.

The last year of actual childhood was the beginning of my upcoming dark ages. I listened to rap around the age of 7 or 8, but it all depends on what type of rap, or just music in general, you listen to, to what sets the mood. This I believe because I can remember numerous times when a simple song pumped me up to just go out and act a fool. Music can be very hypnotic and even influential in my eyes. I can even remember seeing a talk show on TV that had a rap artist named Brotha Lynch Hung who was one of my favorites. The reason they aired him on the show was because a college student had murdered another student while listening to his lyrics. They were just trying to get the point across that music influences, and now so am I. It was in 1992 that I started listening to "hard core" rap with artists using such names as Brotha Lynch Hung, X-raided, ESHAM (East Side Hoes and Money), and NWA (Niggahz With Attitudes) which was tremendously different from what most kids my age were listening to except for that small percentage of juveniles which was the group of people I associated with.

So it was a mixture of music and friends that gave me my introduction to alcohol which slowly progressed to the drug known as marijuana which my era referred to as weed or chronic. Of course there were numerous other names, but those were the most common names I used. I didn't really take a liking to drinking, but I did it more as a social thing than as a real preference of my own. I knew my mom smoked weed because I stole it from her on many occasions, unknown to her. She was funny about it though. She didn't want me doing it or bringing it in the house. She even got mad at me if she smelled it on me. My mom wasn't some kind of addict though, she was a high school English teacher who was naturally stressed and protective of family safety and health. I didn't know my mom used the drug simply to calm her nerves before she would meditate. All I knew is she smoked it, my friends smoked it, and that it wasn't much of a pressure to start the habit myself.

I liked going to school, (for socializing, not educational purposes) but I started skipping a lot so I'd have more free time to do what I wanted. It started out how most things start out, small and not often. I learned the trait in the 5th grade from my friend Josh. He would always ask me if I wanted to play hookey (skip school) but I would always decline because there was no way I could get away with it without my mom finding out. Josh's mom didn't really care so he did it frequently. I used to wish I had a mom like his because it seemed as if he could do whatever he wanted, having his mom's approval at all times. If I wanted to stay the night at a friend's house I had to ask at least a day in advance, if not two. Josh, on the other hand, could call his mom at 11:00pm and say that he'll be staying the night at my house. I had a lot of friends with such privileges which only made me want to grow up faster to attain more "freedom." Although, as I became older, I found my mom to be a much more reliable source, in terms of such things as transportation and money for school clothes.

However, when I got to the 7th grade I also found that all I had to do was erase the message my school would leave on our answering machine and my mom would never know. I also forged my mom's signature on well over 300 detention slips in which I served under 20 of them. I guess they thought if you were bold enough to come to the front office and return a signed detention slip, then you would not try to skip because your parent was already informed, which mine wasn't. I thought they took roll call for detention when you turned the slip in to the office so I would give it to them first thing in the morning and be gone right after the lunch period. I probably only went to school the whole day twice a week. Most of the time I'd come to school high and get too tired and leave halfway through the day.

Towards the end of my 7th grade year when I turned 13 I stopped smoking weed before I came to school and started finishing out the whole day. Mainly because the girlfriends that I had wanted me to. I guess so they could see more of me. I took their advice, but it still didn't help my grades. I was getting straight F's and didn't care, and in reality I had no need to care, because middle school didn't matter. You could get straight F's and still go to high school. Even though I was on the honor roll the year before, I just figured if it really didn't matter, then what was the point. Why should I waste my time with school work, using my effort, when I could just have fun and the same thing would happen in the end. That's how I figured things, but at the end of my 8th grade year I wasn't even enrolled in a school.

My first teenage year was one of my most memorable years. It was where everything happened at once, where I developed into something known as "America's Nightmare." I started off the year fresh, gaining major popularity at school almost instantaneously. Something happened in the summer between my 7th and 8th grade years. I call it my crossover. My mom called it my rites of passage. My first day of school for the 8th grade was different. I had a whole new style about myself and everybody around me could see it, it was visual.

I was making new friends quick and was getting more looks and compliments from females. One girl in particular I remember was Emily. I had known her since kindergarten, but I didn't really "know" her until the 5th grade. We had always been friends, but she used to kinda make fun of me when we were younger. Now all of a sudden she was eyein' me down, askin' how I got so fine. And I'll admit, I was kinda' wonderin' the same thing about her. Then I saw her at a little birthday slumber party a couple of days later. She was already on my agenda so I was glad she was there, because she was what was making the party fun to me. I asked her if she was going to stay for the slumber part of the party. She said something about going to a different party that night and how it would have alcohol and all that. I tried to sway her to stay for the night, not knowing how I myself was going to be able to stay, but she was convinced that she would have a better time at the other party. I'm not trying to say if she would have just listened to me she'd still be alive, but then again, maybe that is what I'm trying to say. No matter how you look at it, she's gone and I can't change the past.

It turned out it was one of my own friends who accidentally shot Emily in the face with a .25 caliber semi-automatic pistol. I couldn't really believe it. No words came to my mouth when my mom told me the news the next morning, that Emily, someone who I had known for over half my life and had deep feelings for had been killed last night at a party that I had tried to talk her out of going to. I went upstairs to my bedroom and cried out tears of frustration, anger, and sadness. When I was finished, I set off some old bottle rockets I had saved from the 4th and vowed never to care for a female like that again. Some people may have known her as a stuck-up bitch, but when she departed from the physical plane it hurt my heart, and I wouldn't allow myself to be hurt like that again.

I remember riding around on my bike right afterwards and telling people in the neighborhood what had happened the previous night. "Fuck her, the stupid bitch deserved it," is what a boy named Jorge told me as we were slowly riding by each other. It made me mad, although I didn't demonstrate my aggressive anger. I just kinda kept riding in shocked realization of being in a cold new world. It nudged me back into the harsh reality I was living in and made me remember that people just don't give a fuck. Later on I found out that Emily was still alive, but in a comma and critical condition. She ended up dying months later at the hands of her mother in a mercy killing which was a weird twist and a whole different story. I tried to shake it all off like nothing had happened, but the truth is, it had changed me even though I wasn't consciously aware of it at the time. Anyhow, that was the first week of a whole year to come living in the shadows of death.

A couple of weeks later, I met someone who came to be one of my best friends. His name was Thomas. Thomas was Filipino and white, but was predominately Filipino. He was hella' funny, like myself, and was also the same age as me, so we got along pretty good. It seemed as if I had known him my entire childhood, when in actuality I had just met him weeks earlier. I quickly became aquainted with his brother Khalil, who was a few years older than Thomas and I, but "kicked it" with us on occasion. Khalil had a lot of the same characteristics as Thomas, but he was a little bit more violent in terms of fighting. Always looking for a bout.

One day myself, Thomas, and his brother Khalil went to the local 7-11 to buy some nachos and slushies. I still remember the somewhat sunny day with its ever so often breeze that quietly blew by. The 7-11 store was on the corner of Indiana and Washington streets, an extremely busy intersection. It was also across the street from my future high school and only three blocks from my residence, so I shopped there frequently, mostly to play the arcade games. While Thomas and Khalil were getting their nachos and slushies, I was on the other side of the store playing a video game called Mortal Kombat. I noticed an older Native American dude come in, probably in his late-30s. He walked past me saying some disrespecting phrases like, "you little punk, you ain't nothing but a gangster puke," and things to that effect. I usually carried a knife on me, but it was just one of those days when I happened not to be armed. I didn't say anything to him, just kind of gave him the evil eye. Thomas and Khalil didn't hear what he had said to me, but they had seen him saying something and asked what it was he had said. I told them it was nothing, just some crazy fool. After the native had walked out of the store we pretty much forgot about it.

When we walked out of the store I got on my bike and started eating my nachos while Thomas and Khalil stood there waiting. Now all of a sudden there was two of them, and I guess they were waiting for us because they abruptly got out an old red pick-up truck and started running at the mouth again. Actually only one of them was talking shit, the same one that was in the store. The other one was just standing there holding a rambo knife in his hand pointing it towards the ground while holding it on the side of his left leg. His face was pretty scarred up and it looked like he may have been mentally disturbed. The truck they had gotten out of had years of rust under the wheel wells and on the side of the fender as well. The rims were black with filth, the tires showing no tread whatsoever. Garbage cluttered the dash and the windshield had numerous chips and cracks in it, rendering the driver's view impaired. A dingy blue tarp obscured the view of what was probably debris or trash in the bed of "old red." By the time I was done analyzing this, which was roughly 8 seconds, I looked over and saw the other one standing pretty close to me.

"Look at you. On your nice bike, with your new clothes. You think you're hot shit, don't you. Well, you ain't nothin but a gangster puke," is what the crazy native dude was mumbling.

I still didn't say anything. I was just wondering how I had provoked this. After about 5 seconds of silence the native man grabbed my nachos and slammed them into my face almost hard enough to knock me off my bike. Thomas and Khalil helped me get my footing and put my bike down, but by that time the natives were already backing out of the parking lot in "old red." I then went in the 7-11 and washed my face off and just chopped it off as a loss. Even though I was extremely mad, I didn't show it. I just knew I would start carrying some kind of weapon wherever I went, and if I had ever seen that red truck again the moment would have been lethal.

Not even two weeks later I got targeted again. I was walking with my girlfriend at the time, Sandra, two of her friends, Sheila and Diana, and two of my friends, Thomas and Joe. It was probably around 9 pm when we got to Sheila's house. At first we were just standing out in front of the house talking and what not. Then Thomas was like, "Hey look at that car creepin."

It was a little white VW rabbit with black windows. All of us kinda glanced over in time to see the window come down about two inches and a black barrel stick out of the open crevice. Before we could even think to do anything, we heard a loud shot fired and the screeching of spinning tires on asphalt. I had felt something whiz right over my head, and I turned around to see if it had hit anybody. It hadn't, but I found a hole directly over my head in the pillar of the house which was about the size of the holes in three ring binder paper. I was thinking to myself that brass knuckles and knives don't work anymore; what I need is a heater. A strap. A gat. A pistolla. A.K.A. protection and power. I made up my mind. This was the last time anyone was going to target me and walk away from it unharmed.

My new-born thought process had changed my behavior at home. It wasn't hard for my mom to see that things were starting to turn sour in the family life. I didn't like my mom's rules, and she didn't like my take on our family responsibilities and my sudden change of demeanor. I thought I was grown and should go by my own rules. Adults and structure wasn't for me. My mom saw it the other way around so I just decided to leave without telling her. I decided to go live with some other juveniles that were on the same road I was on. I moved in with an older dude named Mark.

Mark was two years older than me, was white, and was my sister's X-boyfriend. His house was at was a little more ghetto (broken down) than mine, but because there was nobody telling me what to do, I was straight. Even though Mark's mom was living there and paying the rent, she didn't care that four underage delinquents were living there, just as long as the dishes got done once a week. And the two breezies (females) who stayed there took care of that. We also supplied his mom with money for hard liquor for her addiction. It was more of a partnership though because she would get us all the alcohol we wanted as well. I sold small quantities of crack cocaine to cover my costs at first, but then I found a way to just take money straight out of my bank account which my mom had been forming for me since I was a baby. It was for my future college expenses. I didn't care about college though, plus I found it much easier dealing with bank tellers than base heads.

I had already had a gun for a while, the kind that had killed Emily, and was walking around like a human time bomb. I had pulled the gun on a couple of people who had attempted to threaten me. One time it was a group of about 8 or 10 racist white dudes who threatened to "beat my nigger ass." When I pistol whipped the closest one to me and pointed the rest down with the small barrel of the .25 caliber I had in hand, they all seemed to change their mind for some reason. Even though I didn't spend too much time with my friend Junior (the one who taught me hookey) I heard he was doing the same stuff. He had recently gotten his knuckles blown off in a drive-by and had supposedly shot someone in the face at a fair.

It didn't seem too abnormal of a life since I was surrounded by these sorts of things on a daily basis. The people I knew and hung around with were doing much more than me in terms of criminal activity. It still seemed like I was living in two worlds though, because I still faithfully went to school, and that was entirely different from the living environment I was in. At school I was a regular teen again with all my little friends and my little top notch "girlfriend." When I got away from school premises I was a whole different person. I had different, older friends and was experimenting with sex with other girls who I referred to as "bitches." Sometimes it felt as if I was leading a double life.

I ended up getting picked up by the police while staying at Mark's place. I guess someone had told the police that there were some runaways living at the residence. They only picked up two of the four runaways though, myself and a girl named Kim.

Kim said, "Nice going, Simeon," when she saw the cop pull a handgun out of my pocket.

I felt like slamming her head into the hood of the car, but was restrained by handcuffs at the time. I ended up getting lucky though because the cop that arrested me was the same cop that occasionally worked at my school and knew who I was, not to mention respected me as well.

"Why do you got a gun on you, Simeon?"

I thought fast and said, "I'm just holding it for someone."

He quickly came with a deal stating, "If you give me a name you'll go home today with no charges."

I weighed the components and decided to give him the name, basically snitch - actually there's no basic about it, it was just straight snitching. It, of course, wasn't without a cause though. The dude I bought it from turned out to be a bitch and acted coo' with me, but turned on me and robbed my house a couple days earlier so I thought,

"All right, I can play dirty too." Anyhow, I got released the same day into the custody of my mom. I ate dinner, and then returned to Mark's house hours later.

A couple days later my mom came and picked me up while I was at school and said we needed to talk. We got in her car and went on a ride. After driving about two miles and discussing nothing, I got an eerie feeling that we were headed to the airport, but I had know idea why. I was right, we were going to the airport. When my mom popped the trunk and I discovered every article of clothing already packed in suit cases, I knew exactly why I was there and where I was going. My mom didn't even have to say that I was catching a plane to Oakland to go live with my dad and that maybe I'd straighten up down there, because I already knew what she was thinking.

I didn't run this time, I just accepted it. My dad lived across the tunnel from Oakland in Alameda which wasn't too bad of an area. I made friends quickly and managed to get on my dad's and step-mom's nerves within a couple of weeks. I talked to my mom on the phone a lot and promised to be good if she let me come home. So in six short weeks, I was back home to Spokane, everything back to normal minus a good relationship that couldn't make it over the phone for that long.

This time I calmed down for about a month, still hanging around the same crowds, just not on a daily. One night, I decided to go out to a party with my homeboy, Kevin. Kevin was about 3 years older than me and somewhat of an influence. Kevin usually played it coo' and collected, but everyone that kicked it with him knew not to piss him off because he could be extremely violent at times. Although I never saw him carry any guns, I remember plenty of occasions when I saw him pull a machete out and swing it wildly at unwanted onlookers. It seemed like something always popped off when I was with Kevin. So I liked to kick it with him. I was just careful not to piss him off.

So Kevin and I drove up to the party with his older cousin Joe as our chauffeur. The party was on hit. Everybody got drunk and high including myself. I knew I wasn't going to get home that night but I didn't want to tell my mom.

My homeboy Kevin said, "That's fucked up, you should at least call and tell her."

So I did. I called and told her I wouldn't be coming home to-night. She asked when I'd be coming home, but I just hung up the phone. When I looked back in on instances like this it astounds me on how insensitive and cruel I was and how much pain I put my mother through. The pain now strikes through my heart when I reminisce on such things.

I was gone for a couple of weeks this time. I stuck with Kevin and Alex because Alex was 18, had his own car, and a fake ID that allowed him to buy alcohol. My mom cancelled the access I had to my bank account so I wrote false checks to buy food and scammed three different Hasting Music Stores by buying over $300 of CD's from each store with bad checks. I would then go back to the store the next day with a crumpled up receipt and a faulty story; telling the cashier about how I had spent all my birthday money on these CD's. I told them that my mom had gotten mad at me and that I had to return them and get my money back. The receipt said they were paid for by check, but I ripped that part off and told them I had to dig it out of the garbage. When they asked how I had paid for it I'd state again, "with my birthday money, cash."

With the money that I hustled I bought another gun, a nine millimeter this time, from Alex, and all kinds of jewelry and clothes including a couple of pagers. After staying at a motel for a week just kickin back and layin' low, I went back to school and got all kinds of questions from all the homies and girlies. I was iced out with dia-monds and gold, pagers and way too expensive clothes. Alex even let me roll his Imapla sometimes. Now I thought I was the shit, like that crazy Indian had said months earlier, I thought I was "doin' somethin'."

During all this bouncing around I still managed to make it to school almost every day. Around the middle of April I got into some trouble at school and was expelled but managed to get a teacher ex-pelled from the district as well. About the same time, my mom joined some parents' group called Tough Love. She started pullin' some tricky shit and told me I could either go to a place called CRC (Crisis Resi-dential Center) or have my dad come up and take custody of me again. I picked the third choice; leave the house right now and don't come back. I had no idea why my mom was trying to be so hard core now. I didn't want to join some crisis place, or live in California so I told my mom to have my dad come up and get me, while having no real intention of going back to Cali with him.

My mom made a call and my dad showed up the next morning at 11am. I gave my dad a hug then said I had to go get my bags upstairs. My dad caught me off guard, because I was planning on leaving before he got there. It didn't really matter though because I just bounced out of my sister's bedroom window and climbed up on top of a church roof a block away from my house and just watched the area. Later on I found out my dad went looking for me at some of my friends' houses that my mom had told him about, but eventually he had to drive back home empty handed. I now tremendously regret making my dad waste all that time and energy driving over 30 straight hours for nothing, but at the time I could care less.

That same night I sneaked back in the house through my window and went to sleep. I woke up with the opening of my bedroom door and my mom saying get up and get out. I said I didn't want to and that I wanted to live at home again. She said that if that's what I wanted to do then I had to go to CRC, and so I agreed. I got up and got dressed. I didn't want to leave my gun in my room so my mom could find it, so I took it with me. My mom watched, as I walked out the back door and into the alley. I headed towards the bus stop which was about two blocks away. I walked as slow as I could, wondering where I went wrong. I thought it was just a coincident when the bus rolled up at the exact moment I stepped out of the alley at the bus stop. I don't even think the bus driver knew I was going to get on the bus. He just stopped so someone could get off. I didn't even slow down or speed up, I just walked straight out of the alley and up the stairs of the bus with the same pace. Now I know all things happen for a reason, there is no coincidence.

I got off the bus downtown and found the residence 6 blocks later. I felt pretty odd standing at the front door explaining why I was there with a 44 revolver in my waist band. They took a polaroid of me and admitted me. I asked to use the bathroom and stuck my gun up in the light fixture and left it for my whole two-week stay. It was kind of weird living in huge old house with about ten other kids and getting along. It was a lot like a group home, although it was co-ed, so it was a little different. CRC ended up getting me enrolled in another school and gave me some helpful counseling. My two weeks was up right on my 14th birthday, May 12th, which was a cool present for me.

When I got back home, I chilled out and started going to school. It wasn't that fun for me though since I had to ride the city bus all the way across town and I only knew one girl at the whole school. After doing this for two weeks I somehow lost all three of my bus passes. I had one for the month I was on and the other two were for the next two months to come. I didn't want to tell my mom I lost them so I just stopped going to school without her knowing. I figured it wouldn't matter since I only took three classes a day and there were only two weeks left until summer.

I was still staying out of trouble though, until the summer came and everybody wanted to kick it again. I wanted to take it slow and easy, but there were just too many parties and girls happenin'. I couldn't resist getting back into the cycle. This time I didn't get carried away and start leaving home though, I was trying to obey my 1am curfew but it was hard at that age. Females liked me because I had gold and a car. Actually it was my mom's car that I would borrow on occasion. That and my dimples - yeah, right.

So I was rolling around in a new model Honda Accord LX with guns, drugs, money, and girls, parlayin' every night at the age of fourteen almost all behind my mom's back. Soon violence came into play as well. I started getting into fights with all kinds of people I didn't even know almost everywhere I went. Females that had something vulgar to say got the raw end of the stick too. Physical violence became second nature. I had finally lost all of what little conscience I had and was fully aware of it, even boasting it at times.

I continued my low conscious lifestyle through the summer and brought my malice with me for my first year in high school. The first month of school I was suspended for assaulting a boy in between classes and taking his discman. I didn't like the fact that I was now one of the youngest at school and didn't get as much attention as I did the year before, but I was still somewhat known so I stayed with it. I heard some stories about this dude named Corey who had the meanest rep in the district and how if you looked at him for a second too long, you would become a victim. He happened to be going to my school, North Central, was close to 20 years-old and despised all freshman. It also just so happened that he really didn't like me because he thought that I thought I was some kind of bad-ass. I got the hint after he gave me a couple of incoherent messages, so I started carrying a small curved knife with me to school every day.

School was just a social gathering to me. I went for nothing more than meeting up with my friends and whatever female I was going out with. Myself, Thomas, and Khalil, who I now referred to as my cousins because we were so close, and my other good friend Johnathan, would come to school high every day. I knew Johnathan since the 6th grade. He lived one block away from me, so we kicked it a lot of the time. He was a little white dude with red hair, so at first glance you might think he was a square. That is, until he opened his mouth. He could make almost anyone break down and just ball out tears of laughter. He was that funny. That's why I liked him so much. It seemed like I was at his house just about every day. I went through my rites of passage with him, but it didn't seem like he had changed that much, except for the fact that he now smoked weed. And I was the one who introduced him to that. I was there when Thomas took his first hit of the chronic to. And now we were all high, at school, just fuckin' off, not caring about nothin'.

That's what really started messin me up, was not caring about school, my family, my future, and ultimately, myself. I ended up getting expelled from that school as well. The weapon that I had been bringing to school "accidentally" slipped out of my coat pocket when I was leaning back in a chair during my social studies class. I still remember the teacher's name, Mr. Knight, and the look on his face when he saw it land on the floor right below me. I just chopped it up and casually put it back in my pocket. Moments later, I was escorted off the campus by some security people, and was told never to set foot on the premises again.

Only October, and I was already out of school. I stayed home for a couple of weeks and had major people kickin at my house while my mom was at work, like my bedroom was some kind of cool class to come to. If it was a class, all we were studying was weed smoke because you couldn't even see the ceiling in my room.

After that got played out, I was enrolled at an alternative school a couple of blocks from my house. Even though I was still smoking chronic I had actually started doing my work since there weren't that many people I knew around me. Of course it didn't last long though. I went to all my morning classes and was doing good, but I was just missing too many afternoon classes.

It's like whenever you get close enough to actually touch something it crumbles into pieces and slides through the spaces between your fingers. It was now probably the month of March, but I can't remember exactly for sure. I didn't let my mom know I was dropped from school until she somehow found out, I think by a notice in the mail. She was upset, but agreed to put me in night school at the same alternative school. I tried to explain that I just wasn't a morning person and I couldn't function as good in the AM hours, so during the day I pretty much slept only to be awakened around noon by my cousin Khalil playing my stereo at high volumes. I'd usually leave the front door open so he could just come in without waking me up so he could cook some food or do whatever. One day he woke me up by shooting a single shot from a 22 caliber pistol with an extended barrel into the side of my metal garbage can penetrating it and sending the bullet slamming into the wall by my dresser.

"Wake up, dog. Peep this new strap I just got," Khalil said, as if what he had just done was not abnormal.

"Man, what the fuck is wrong with you," I responded in a sleepy but pissed off voice. "The neighbors could've heard that shit."

"Man, shut up with that shit, dog. You wanna buy this shit or what, $70."

I had gotten rid of all my other guns, so I ended up buying it for $50. I sanded it down and made it look brand new. I liked the gun so much I started carrying it everywhere I went. The daytime was starting to get real played out so I met up with this dude named Dan. He was a white dude, but he knew how to pull some cold licks (robberies). His and mine styles were almost identical and our mentality was pretty much the same too. We started going out during the day and pulling little jack moves here and there. Then all of a sudden, it was summer again and everybody wanted to party.

Some shit started poppin' off and the next thing I knew was that I hadn't been home in about four days. I was parlayin' with my homie Lou and just got sucked into some drastic shit. I met Lou in the 7th grade. He was in a grade lower than me but he was only a month younger than me in age. Lou was a rowdy mutha' fucka', always gettin' into some type of trouble. If you wanted to stay out all night parlayin' then you stayed at his house, because there wasn't no rules over there.

It was at Lou's house that we threw a party where I got twisted (drunk) for my first time. It was at Lou's house that bitches would come over and get they freak on. And it was at Lou's house that Robert Pearson was arrested for the shooting of Emily. And now I woke up at his house with a hangover thinking, "Damn, I gotta go home and get my stuff and talk to my mom."

By the time I got home, my mom was so mad she didn't even talk. When I said I was just going to shower, get some clothes and leave, she flashed (lost her temper) on me cold. She demanded that I go with her and my sister to Idaho to visit her friend for three days. I just chopped it up and left town with them. While we were in Idaho, I stole her friend's 20 gauge shotgun and took it back with me, unnoticed, to Spokane.

Lou suggested I just move in with him, and I, of course, thought it was a good idea - more freedom for me. The house itself was uncomfortably small and extremely ghetto. You could literally smell the welfare reeking throughout the interior. The exterior was equivalent to that of a crack house. Lou's mom usually wore a black eye from what we assumed to be the doing of her boyfriend - I mean, how many times did she expect us to believe that she ran into a door? The house could be pretty hectic at times, but there weren't too many rules us teens had put with.

All we had to do was go get all my stuff at the house, which turned out to be not so easy. We made the trip when my mom was, of course, gone and started putting all my stuff in a oversized green duffle bag, including all my mom's hard liquor. We walked out the front door, which was a big mistake. Lou was carrying the duffle bag and my VCR and I was carrying my TV with the cord dangling in mid air behind.

We missed the first bus by about thirty seconds. It must have looked pretty funny to see two guys trying to run down the street with TVs and VCRs in their hands. We trekked about 5 blocks because of running after the bus and backtracking. I don't know what the bus driver was thinking when he saw us standing there at the bus stop, but he pulled up and opened the doors. Lou got on first, paid then sat down. Just as I dropped my last piece of change into the machine a DARE van pulled up and stopped right in front of the bus while about five other unmarked police cars blocked off the surrounding intersections.

I was standing there dumbstruck. The cop approached the door of the bus, gun drawn.

"Leave the TV and walk slowly backward, down the stairs, with your hands on the back of your head," was Officer Grant's demand.

Officer Grant was a big man of African American decent. Standing at around '6 "4 and weighing well over 250 lbs., he usually puts the suspect at somewhat of a disadvantage. Although his natural personality was as friendly as Mr. Rogers, his solid rock-like demeanor made you want to cooperate. I did what he said.

"Where's your buddy?" was his next question.

"I don't have no buddy. I'm by myself," I responded, but it wasn't hard for them to spot Lou with a big green bag and a VCR because they, of course, had descriptions of us both.

A different cop cuffed me and took me back to my house in the back of a squad car. My mom was out in the front yard with a disgusted look on her face. She started yelling at the cop to charge me with everything that they could and to send me away for the longest time that was possible. When the cop got back in the car, I was eager to tell him all about my mom and her marijuana habit. You could almost here the clap, clap of my gums flapping away as I spilled the entire can of beans. In actuality I was just venting because I was so mad at what my mom had said.

But the cop just laughed and said, "Oh, now you want to talk. Before, you said that you didn't have anything to say."

"Well, I do now." I said, "All you got to do is go look and see if I'm lying."

"Hey, why don't you just keep it down back there, I'm tired of listening to your mouth," was his response.

I ended up getting lucky again though. My arresting officer, Officer Grant, was my DARE officer in the 6th grade and he remembered my good behavior fairly well. Somehow I escaped punishment, and was again released the same day without any charges. But, as usual, I didn't learn from the lenience and was out running amok in no time.

And it was virtually days later that I was caught stealing a car. Me and Dan were out roaming around the south hill (the wealthy part of Spokane) and saw a brand new Mazda MX6 in a Domino's parking lot. The door was slightly ajar with the keys dangling from the ignition. It was ours, we were on it faster than "a fat bitch who sat down too fast." We were more than happy when we discovered over 600 dollars cash in the glove box ($643 to be exact). After that, Dan left the car alone while my dumb ass went driving it around with females for about a week or so. Anyhow, I ended up getting in a high speed chase with the police while four anonymous girls were in the car. I saw an unmarked slowly following me, so I dipped off. It was a little too late when one of the girls said, "Hey man, just take me home."

I ended up smashing around a corner going 60 mph and hitting a big block of wood in someone's front yard and spinning into a parked car. I was already hopping over a fence, fleeing from the owner of the parked car and his pit bull before the girls could even unbuckle their seat belts. The police found me about a half a mile away in another car that was in a garage by using their K9 dogs. I was lucky enough to be inside a car so I didn't get bitten up, although they quickly roughed me up and threw me into the, now familiar, back seat of a police car. A cop drove me back to the car wreck scene just in time for me to hear the dude with the pit bull threaten to kill me if he ever saw me again.

The police wanted the money from the car, but I told them I had spent it all. They didn't believe me even though it was very likely that I had. The crime was minor to the jail so they let me go after holding me for about three hours. I went home with my Mom and ate some left over KFC for a late dinner. I still felt good. I had gotten away again.

I cooled down for a second and started stealing mountain bikes out of people's garages up on the south hill. It was just for fun at first, but then Dan knew this guy who would give $200 for a decent brand named mountain bike with front suspension. So we made it a full time job clearing $600 on a good day. A lot of my other friends were making about the same or more, selling dope (crack cocaine), but as a juvenile I had a lot more fun going places and getting my adrenaline running. On my way home with a bike that I had just stolen, Dan and I would also break into cars and put anything worth stealing in the good ol' Jansport backpack. Sometimes people liked to try and chase us off so I usually stayed strapped (carried a gun) during my crosstown treks.

One night when I was riding home by myself, the chain on my

bike snapped when I went off a curb. It was something that happened on occasion, so I casually turned the bike upside down, and started fixing it. I heard a car coming out of an alley directly across the street from me. When I looked up it shined its brights right in my face. The car was an old Chevrolet two door hatchback. It looked like it had been driven down dirt roads for weeks upon weeks without a single wash. The car's grill was no longer in place and all four tires were without hubcaps. In my definition, it was a smoker's bucket. The car then drove out of the alley and attempted to hit me, but I jumped back, onto the sidewalk. As the car neared the end of the block I stepped out into the street and watched, as it proceeded to flip a bitch. It drove back and passed me slowly and the passenger turned and looked at me, flipping me off with both hands. They made another u'ie at the end of the block and sped back towards me trying to hit me again. I made the same maneuver and then started walking toward the car with my hands up in a "what you wanna do" posture. They stupidly just stayed parked at the end of the block in the middle of the intersection waiting for me.

Before I got to the passenger window, I noticed the dude in the passenger seat doing something between his legs while looking down at whatever it was he was doing. I figured that they didn't know I had walked up on them and were probably loading a gun or something. I thought to myself, "ya should'a been prepared like me." I stood at the passenger door. My palms were a bit moist, and my heart was beginning to beat at a slightly faster pace. The dude in the passenger seat glanced up unexpectedly, looking into the barrel of my Ruger 22 as I rapidly started squeezing the trigger. The car smashed off in a hurry, swerving from side to side almost hitting every parked car on the block as I squeezed off my last two rounds shattering the back window of their car. I hadn't a clue if there were any casualties because everything happened so fast and nothing ever came up on the news. I looked to my right noticing my old elementary school, Garfield, but not a single memory passed through my mind. I just went back home like nothing happened, because at the time, I still had no conscience.

About a week later I got caught with the same gun. I was riding in a car with four of my close homeboys, and with my cousin Khalil's girlfriend, who was driving. To make a long story short, the cops pulled us over and I got booked with the gun. The gun was under the passenger seat, so they never saw it on me, but I had just gotten a statement put on my profile a couple of days ago that stated I was waving a gun around in my neighborhood. The truth was, it was a bee-bee gun that I was waving around. I was just shooting pesky stray cats. It didn't matter though because it looked the same as the other gun and that was all they needed, a similar match in description.

They took me down to the juvenile where I spent three hot summer days on red flag (a 23 in one program - meaning I got one hour out a day and spent the other 23 hours in my room). When I got out I felt like I had done some hard time and started boasting it to people around my neighborhood which they ahhhed me for in utter disbelief. Even though I had been caught and consequented, I felt good, like I had been empowered from the small time I was incarcerated.

The first day of my release I was right back in the hot box. In the back seat of a Jeep Cherokee fleeing from the police in a high-speed chase. "I got mad skillz, son. Peep my drivin abilities, kid," the driver that I didn't know too well was saying.

If you couldn't tell, he was from the Big BA, New York City. He didn't drive as well as he boasted, though, because we ended up parked in someone's living room. All five of us fled on foot, uninjured from the wreck. Everyone got away except one dude who I didn't know and was glad for that, because when he found out how much restitution he would be paying, names would start flying out of his mouth faster than the water that jumps up out of the toilet and into your asshole before it can close. A couple of days later my homeboy Marco smashed a car I had stolen into a cop car going about 80 mph down a side street. He got away because the cop was knocked unconscious in the crash. I was mad because I had left some belongings in the car, but I was also glad that I had been cautious and worn leather gloves during my daily rides in the car. Most people didn't leave home without their American Express. I didn't leave home without my leather gloves.

About a week later I got into another high speed chase with the police. My homeboy Marco was driving and my homeboy Jackson was in the back. Marco was half black, half native and was about the same size as me, 5 '10" - a buck 40. Jackson was half-Mexican, half white, but was a little bit smaller than Marco and I, but we were all the same age. I was telling Marco to use all his signals, blinkers, and brake lights, while he was driving when an unmarked police car started tailing us.

Before he had a chance to flash his overhead lights, I said, "Fuck it, high speed," and Marco instantly hit the gas.

Not only was the vehicle stolen, but we also had a stolen 12 gauge shotgun in the back and all kinds of alcohol, dope and weed on us. So we were more than determined to evade capture.

"Should I turn, should I turn," Marco shouted.

"Nah' man go straight, just keep going straight," Jackson and I shouted back.

Marco for some reason paid no heed to our directions and tried to turn a corner going around 60-70 mph. To help the situation out it was raining at the time, so you can imagine what happened when Marco turned the steering wheel. We luckily went right in between a street sign and a telephone pole missing them by mere inches. If we had hit either it probably would have killed us all on contact. We then smashed through a four-foot chain link fence. The fence actually stopped us before we hit the house because it rose up over the hood and crashed into the windshield. The entire fence uprooted out of the ground until we came to a stop, lightly bumping into the side of the house.

I was extremely intoxicated but sobered up very quickly when the police K9 units started chasing us on foot. It felt like I had been running for miles- I could feel Easy-E when he made the album "100 miles and running." I must have hid in 20 different places, but the K9 kept close on my trail. I finally just gave up and jumped into some thorn bushes when I saw the cops had the entire area I was in completely blocked off. I wasn't too hard of a target to spot since I was dressed in all white. When the K9 walked right past me, I remembered that dogs had no distinction between colors except for the color red. When the dog backtracked, making a second pass at me, my heart started beating rapidly. The K9 sniffed past me again, then turned around and came my way once more, this time bumping into my shoe with his nose. I flinched and teeth immediately sunk in. I still had my leather gloves on so I grabbed the dog's mouth and flipped him on his back. The K9 yelped and was instantly on all fours again, this time mangling my legs in a ferocious frenzy. I attempted to grab the dog's mouth again but was interrupted by a 9mm glock tapping the back of my head.

"Get up! Get up now!" the cop yelled.

"I can't man. The dog won't let go," I helplessly replied.

"Get the fuck up now! I'm gonna' blow your fucking head off!" Mr. Glock screamed.

"I can't!" I pleaded, "The dog got me. The dog got me!"

Another cop grabbed the back of my neck and yanked me out of the thorn bushes, the K9 still attached to my leg, his head still shaking wildly. A knee then flew sharply into the small of my back enforced with a few hundred pounds.

"We got two of you. Where's your other buddy?" the cop inquired.

"Get the fuckin' dog off me, man. He's fuckin' my leg up," I exhaled.

They finally pulled the dog off of me after he didn't respond to three different commands. They let me up and read me my rights.

"No comment," I said.

"Watch your head," the cop said as he slammed my dome piece into the car door frame. "Hey, you should be more careful in handcuffs. Oh, well. You're going to the hospital anyways."

I went to the hospital and got my legs bandaged up. I sat there handcuffed to the bed rail listening to some guy who was behind a curtain screaming his lungs out. The cop told me that the guy had gotten stabbed through the back of his neck with a knife. After the stabbing victim's cries fell silent, the cop uncuffed my wrists from the bed rail. I then learned that my homeboy Marco, the last one to be caught, was a lot worse off than me. The K9 that had gotten him had made sure that he wasn't getting away because Marco couldn't even walk for about two weeks. Ironically, the dog's name was Zeus. After the cop told me about everyone getting caught, he drove me back to my second home, juvenile hall.

This time I didn't get out the same day, though. I should have gotten out in 30 days, 15 for the car I had stolen and 15 for the gun, but I found out that they were going to manifest injustice (go outside the standard range) and give me 65 weeks. I also found out that my homeboy Josh was in there for two first degree murders and two attempted murders. During my trial they used that against me saying that I idolized Josh for what he had done and that I was a complete menace to the society.

They found me guilty, and I was sent to Naselle youth camp in

November '95. I tried to act good and got on the DNR crew (Department of Natural Resources). We went out with chain saws and cut down trees for $5.00 a day. The hours were long and the work was hard. I was just about to give up when something good happened. Not even two months had went by and my appeal came through. I went back to the Spokane Juvenile and the Judge let me out on special releases. Was it luck again or just bad karma building up?

When I got out I started kickin' it with my girlfriend, which was Liz at the time. She kept me out of trouble for awhile, but she was a bit rowdy herself. After three or so weeks, I hooked back up with Dan and started robbing houses. By now, Dan wasn't even allowed in my house, according to my Mom's rules, but rules were meant to be broken so, of course, Dan was just chillin' over at the house while my Mom was at work. I lost track of time and the next thing I knew, I saw my Mom looking through the window of my bedroom door with the most disgusted face I'd ever seen her wear. She opened the door and started screaming over the already deafening music that was blasting out of my boss surround sound stereo that I had just stolen hours earlier from a house on the south hill.

"Get out of my house right now. I am just furious with you, Simeon," my mom yelled after I turned the music off.

"All right," I said, "if you wanna be all mad and rude, I'll just leave too."

So Dan, Liz, and I left in a hurry and went downtown. While I was at the bus plaza I saw this one dude who I knew as Delux. Delux was just a little darker than me in complexion so I assumed he was mulatto, like myself. He was probably around 6'2", about twenty years old and had long hair that was kept in braids. I had met Delux at a pool hall called The Underground.

Now we were all at the bus plaza and Delux was clowning on Liz because she was wearing both the legs of her sweat pants up on her knees instead of the present fad which was one pant leg up and one down.

"You ain't from no east coast girl, you betta' take yo' ass home," Delux clowned.

"This ain't no east coast style," Liz said. "They be sportin' their sweats like this in Cali, ask Evil, he know."

She was referring to me when she said Evil, because that was my alias, Lil Evil, and I knew what she said was true, but I responded with, "Shit, I don't know what chu' talkin' 'bout."

Then I remember Delux saying in these exact words, " 'ey, man, whatever you do, don't go out there and do somethin' stupid."

I said, "Aiight." But didn't take his advice.

Some other dude was talking major head to me and Dan inside the plaza, but I quieted him with a flash of what looked like a glock in a shoulder holster, but was actually a police nightstick in the sleeve of my leather coat. Dan had the real gun. I didn't want to carry any more guns because I was on parole and knew another gun charge would be close to two years. So I sometimes carried a nightstick around for my protection. The coat I carried it in was pretty big so you couldn't see any abnormal bulkiness.

Liz, Dan, and I caught a bus up to the south hill and kicked it at a little multi-shopping-restaurant center called Lincoln Heights. We lost track of the time, and it started getting late. I kept saying I should catch a bus and go home, but we all kept ignoring my words, just staying longer. Then as we were on our way to the bus stop we saw the bus roll by, the last bus of the night.

Our choices were slim. We could either walk home, which was about four miles in February sub-zero degree weather or we could steal the Suburban that was sitting in the pizza parlor parking lot, running, with no one in it. We chose the second option because we knew none of our parents would come get us. All the doors were locked, so I bashed the back passenger window out with my nightstick and unlocked the driver door with one swift motion. Dan was supposed to run up and get in the driver's seat, but for some reason he went to the front passenger side. There was no time for me to say anything about it because we could see the owner frantic, running through the pizza parlor trying to get to the front door. I jumped in and unlocked Dan's door so he could get in. It was all dark in the Suburban so I couldn't see what gear I was shifting and the truck kept bouncing forward as I was trying to find reverse. Meanwhile, the owner was pounding on Dan's window trying to open his door yelling at us to get out. Liz had tried to get in the door that I had smashed the window out of but was unsuccessful due to a malfunction of the lock so she ran behind the pizza parlor before the owner saw her. I finally found reverse and smashed out of there in a hurry, accidentally running over the owner in the process.

The deal was that if anyone didn't get in the car on time that we'd meet up with them at the Safeway underground parking lot which was four blocks away. Well, I was the one driving and I was kinda' paranoid so I went straight downtown. I wasn't even a block into the downtown area when a police car hit his overhead lights. I pulled over and waited for the cop to get out of his car. He didn't, so I figured he was calling for backup and vamped (disappeared) on him. We almost got away, but when I went off a one foot curb the engine stalled on us and the cops swooped us up. I still didn't care though. I was laughing uncontrollably for the whole five-mile chase. I just wanted to give them a run for their money, which I did.

I got out of the truck first, hands up, infra-red beams targeting my back. Dan wasn't the good friend I thought he was because I was mysteriously charged with: SECOND DEGREE UNLAWFUL POSSESSION OF A FIREARM, to wit: a .25 caliber pistol. I tried to tell the cop that I didn't mess with straps (guns) anymore, but he wouldn't listen to me after I had already declined on making a statement. It wasn't until later that I read Dan's testimony in the police report. It disgusted me when I read a statement saying that he had seen me with the gun earlier.

While I was in the juvenile looking at exactly what I had said earlier, 22 months, just under two years, the police had linked the gun found under my seat to the house where it had come from. So there came another charge of first degree burglary which gave me an additional two years minimum. Then to top that off, some detectives searched my bedroom at my house, seized some credit cards and linked them to another first degree burglary. The domino effect kept going because an assault rifle had been stolen from that house, although they never found it. Now all of a sudden, I was looking at close to six years. I was still insouciant though, showing no signs of recognition whatsoever. I simply planned to skip all those years by escaping.

I waited for my court dates to go by before I escaped to make sure I was really going to get all that time. While I was waiting I met this beautiful Italian girl named Carmela who I quickly started to get feelings for. We both had relationships on the streets, but we lied to each other, saying that we didn't. I found out when I came up behind her and snatched a picture of her boyfriend out of her hands and inquired, "Who is this?" She found out when Liz came in to the juvenile for a TMV (stealing a car) and almost killing her friend Tiffany by smashing into a tree in a high speed police chase. I broke up with Liz before she found out about Carmela, but Carmela found out about it because of rumors that quickly spread around the juvenile. Carmela started acting funny, but we resolved our differences.

One night while I was laying in my bed trying to figure out what love was all about and if I loved Carmela in that certain way, this extremely powerful sensation over came me. All the wrong I had done and all the people I had hurt came flooding through my whole body at once. Tears swelled up in my eyes and mental pain flowed through every vein that interlaced my body. I felt all the regret and the guilt and pain I had caused at the same time. And then, just as fast as it came, it was gone and I felt nothing once again. I thought that there might have been something wrong with me because for about thirty seconds I had had some sort of strange encounter, but I soon forgot about the incident.

On the night I was planning to escape, I severely sprained my ankle playing basketball in the gym. If I put so much as a pound of pressure on it, pain shot through my whole lower leg. I was more mad than anything. I didn't even tell the nurse about it. I just tried to hide my limp. The next day I came down with an extremely high fever and blacked out in the shower. I had to call it off for the time being. My plans were cancelled.

Carmela got out, and I lost contact with her immediately. Although I still had deep feelings for her and still do, I just had to chop it up, because; life goes on. I had my sixteenth birthday in the juvenile then got sent back up to Naselle nine days later to finish my juvenile life sentence. I didn't do too good up there though. I refused to get on the DNR (Department of Natural Resources) crew because I didn't like the woods and the chain saw. They also didn't let people choose roommates, and they roomed me up with a skinhead so I tied my sheet into a knot and whipped him in the face until he started crying. Instead of telling the staff that I had hurt him, he fabricated up a false story, saying that I was planning on brutally assaulting staff and escaping. The staff didn't even listen to what I had to say. They just immediately put me in isolation, until they transported me to the Maple Lane School a couple of days later.

When I got to Maple Lane I just chilled out and acted like a model resident. I roomed up with my old homie from Spokane. His name was Ronnie. We use to be roommates in the juvenile until he left to Maple Lane about a week before I went to Naselle in November of '95. Ronnie was the same age as me, two months older, about the same height and weight and was mixed like me as well. Our taste in attire was more than somewhat similar, we cracked the same cuts (listened to the same music), and we both pretty much stayed to ourselves, trying not to get caught up in the dramatized bullshit that circulated throughout the institution on a daily. To stay out of the housing unit and out of trouble we took a culinary arts class that enabled us to work at the Central Kitchen for 40 hours a week. We got into a little trouble, quickly received our honor level and just kicked back and stayed away from the staff. I only talked to the staff when necessary, such as getting phone calls or packages open, basically getting my needs met. Even though I was being good and staying out of trouble I still had a strong disliking for authority figures.

Ronnie got out after serving a little over a year. I had a tattoo on my left forearm that said Lucky, but I always thought Ronnie was the one who was lucky because his rap sheet (criminal record) was definitely bigger than mine and all he got was 13 months, while his victim ended up dying in the hospital. I started meeting a lot of people who were locked up for murder and were doing considerably less time than me. I saw how crooked the system really was and wondered why I was serving a juvenile life sentence for a couple of property crimes when other people were doing three years for shooting people in the face. So I rationalized and justified my crimes and devised a master plan to gain the staff's trust and then to escape when they least expected it.

I should have been a junior in high school and just getting a driver's license, but instead, I had zero credits and was learning about other people's crimes and what went wrong with them. Instead of going to the school they had in Maple Lane, I switched around to different jobs, starting out in their central kitchen and then moving to their labor crew which took us off campus into the community for four days a week.

Before I knew it, a year had gone by and I was 17. It was pretty weird looking back and seeing how much I had done when I was 15 and comparing it to how little I had done during my 16th year. The only thing really significant that happened during my 17th year was when I pulled off my master plan. My roommate, Sun, and I were both disgusted with the system. Sun was 17 years old and was doing the same J-life stretch of time I was doing. Sun was about 5'7" and pretty rocked up from the weight room. Even though his crime dealt with robbery and assault, he was a very respectful and calm person. The only time I saw him get angry was when someone said something disrespectful about his race, which was Cambodian. Sun was the most well behaved resident on campus. He had two jobs and had graduated from high school a year early. Everyone was sure that they would let him go to a group home early. When they denied him community placement, he decided to join me with my escape plot.

Both myself and Sun had been on a number of off-campus honor trips (an escorted outing into the community with no restraints while wearing regular street clothes), so they didn't expect us to bolt across the street in downtown Seattle and disappear into a crowd of 60,000 people after watching a football game at the Kingdome. And this we did easily. We left Seattle and went to Tacoma the same night, by hitching a ride from some GI's. We then called one of Sun's friends who came and picked us up from the Tacoma Mall and brought us to his hometown of Cle Elum. We laid low there for ten days managing to have way too much fun and avoiding potential arrests by the local police twice.

We got some dividends from Sun's homeboy and caught the Greyhound to Spokane. Despite the long hot ride on the bus I was feeling pretty good. "You can't keep me locked down, bitch!" is what I screamed out, after walking a couple of blocks away from the bus station.

While I was still at Maple Lane I had gotten back together with Liz through writing letters, so I called her house, but her friend Sherry informed me that she was parlayin' in the City of Las Vegas. I asked Sherry if I could stay there until Liz got back, but her dad didn't want anyone over there because his house had been raided days earlier by the Task Force on some unrelated drug shit. Since her house was hot, Sherry said I could stay at her friend's apartment which I did for about a week. Her friend ended up being Ronnie's (my old roommate) baby's mom. Ronnie and I reminisced on some old school things and had some fun.

Then Liz came back from Vegas and I stayed at her house, even though the spot was hot, for almost three days. I probably would have stayed longer, eventually going down to Vegas with her, but she found out I that I'd had sex with her "good friend" Sherry and dropped me off downtown with a stinging goodbye. I had reason to believe that she was making booty calls on the DL so I thought little of it. From there, I went to my homeboy Johnathan's house and ate up all his hospitality for five days. We really had some laughs talking about, "back in the day." I felt my welcome had run out there so I went to stay with some dudes I knew from middle school. I was pretty surprised when I learned that they had gotten their own apartment. I remembered Cliff as a young neighborhood thug, overweight and stealing bikes out of people's garages. Now he was in shape and flashin' gold and answering pager calls. Evan seemed different too, in fact, everybody did. I didn't even recognize a girl that I'd known since the 7th grade, while she stood right in front of me. Cliff and Evan basically sold different types of drugs, mainly weed, for a living, so they didn't care, to a certain extent, how long I stayed there. Just as long as I kicked some dough down (give them some money) every once in a while. During all this, Sun was still with me so it kind of made things harder.

We didn't stay at the apartment for too long though, because we were re-captured by the authorities during a raid by the police. It wasn't a drug raid, though. They were looking specifically for Sun and me, because someone told the detectives that we had something to do with a murder that had happened in the area. The tables turned for the worse this time. We were taken downtown and booked for first degree escape and suspicion of murder.

I spent over 100 long days and nights stressing the murder charge in the county jail. My public "pretender" was riding my ass saying I'd better cooperate with the police if I really didn't have anything to do with the murder and to take a polygraph (lie detector) test. I finally took my lawyers advice, getting my name cleared while Sun was indicted on first degree aggravated murder charges. But by clearing my name I also had to agree to testify against Sun. The police were playing me dirty and they knew it. I just hope Sun would overstand that I couldn't spend the rest of my life in a state penitentiary for something I didn't do. A lot of people might have perceived me as a bitch, but the truth is they would have done the same thing in those circumstances. Even though I knew Sun, I didn't "know" Who He Really Was, and until you hop directly into someone else's shoes, they can't be judged. Basically, what I'm saying is that the decision I made was the hardest decision I made in my life, but it was the right one, and until you're able to jump inside my body and experience what I felt, you can't say shit.

I was more than happy to come back to Maple Lane after going through all that, although the administration people were ridiculously disgusted at me. Instead of letting me go to the open campus after my court was done with the escape charge, which I only got 28 days for, they threw me in the IMU (Intensive Management Unit) for over a year. The worst time of my whole sentence was in there, although I also learned quite a few things.

The staff in Birch, the IMU cottage, continually dicked me day after tiring day. I knew they were trying to break me, but I somehow managed to stay on my toes, propelling myself away from the staff's negativity by manifesting a state of mind that resided on another level. A level that the administrators of Maple Lane couldn't touch. My encouragement came mostly from my mom who stuck with me through thick and thin, never giving up hope on me.

———

Through everything I had done years before, if what my mom was showing wasn't unconditional love I don't know what it was. My mom was the greatest supporter, the most caring person and the grandest mother a son could ever have. The faith my mom gave came directly from her heart; she was an extremely strong-minded person. She sought out what she wanted to do in life and executed it. Her dedication towards helping people made her exceed far in life. It was like she could see through the illusions that life sometimes projected, as if she knew all things to be impermanent, as to waste no time grasping and clinging onto the ever-so prevalent materialized world. Never becoming distracted with what life gave her, she always let go and let the process of life work things out. She was open to all ideas. She had a gentle yet commanding nature about her, and was a phenomenal person. She always had the answer to everything and was always there for me when I needed her, she was the realist and from then on, I started giving her all my respect because she deserved it, she deserved it all.

I gained mental flight in Birch and started studying spirituality to get more enlightened as a human being. I also started studying on my schooling. I worked double time and gained over twelve credits during my year in Birch. I was finally released to open campus thirteen long hellish months later. I immediately did exceedingly well and gained level 4 honor status. Open campus was a lot different to me, a lot better. I got along with all the staff and my peers using little effort. I started looking at everything in a new perspective manifesting my own reality into that of a struggle-free one. The administrators refused to give me my honors badge (an ID that let level 4's walk around campus without being supervised by staff) for no particular reason, just personal discrimination stuff. I still didn't let it get to me though. I was now 18, close to adulthood and had to start acting like it. I had to face reality and take responsibility for my own actions, which I did well.

Sometime in March of 1999, I was subpoenaed to the big trial with Sun. I tried to help him out by making myself look guilty because I knew the police couldn't charge me with the crime. I didn't care when Sun testified to the jury that I was the actual murderer although the detective threatened to press charges again because of a new witness saying that I confessed to him about doing the crime. Anyhow, I wasn't charged and the trial soon fell apart for Sun's case during the end when the judge reversed his statement and told the jury Sun's prior offenses. He is now currently serving a mandatory life sentence in Clallum Bay penitentiary with no eligible chance of parole, but still staying in contact with my mom who is supportive of his situation.

I got back to Maple Lane a couple of weeks later and maintained my honor level and my sanity. The summer seemed to roll by worry free. Then, in a shocking phone call in September '99 I received some news that changed things. I was informed that my mother was diagnosed with cancer to the kidney, although her health seemed fine. The disease didn't affect her for the first 5-6 months, so we didn't believe the doctors when they said she had six months to two years left to live. We didn't think it was right for a doctor to scare a person by giving them a death sentence that seemed so unreal.

I then happily graduated from high school with a 3.8 GPA at the late age of 19. I thought it was still good since I had 0 credits at 17. After I had graduated I sought community placement at a group home, but the administration screening committee denied my papers stating that I could not be rehabilitated, even though I displayed nothing but adult-like behavior since I had been put in Birch minus a couple of incidents. I guess they were still holding a grudge from 1997 when I had escaped; now who's the adult here, hmmm, I wonder. Anyhow, I took it as another lesson, a life obstacle, something to grow from and a karmic debt. Basically, I just chopped it up as life.

Some time in October of '99 I began taking correspondence classes with a program called Gateway, which was facilitated by the Evergreen State College. The program was very unique; in fact, there is no program like it in the country.

Around March of 2000 the symptoms of cancer embedded themselves into the body of my mother with extreme rapidness. My mother had to retire from her job as a teacher, which she didn't mind too much. She was becoming weaker day by day, relying on help from friends and family, although there wasn't too much family to help. My sister had to go off to college at the UW in Seattle because she had already missed her first quarter as a freshman. She still flew down to help when she could, though. My grandma, needing help herself, did what she could to assist my mom in her times of need. My dad stepped in and helped out by making some calls to Maple Lane, and getting them to fly me over to Spokane to visit my mom at her house.

During my eight hour visit with my mom I saw just how badly impaired she was. She couldn't use her right arm and got extremely tired if she sat up too long. It was a good visit, but it wasn't, if you know what I mean. It almost broke my heart to witness my mom in that condition, the strongest figure in my life, and to see the unconditional tears of love swell up in my grandmother's eyes as she hugged me before I left back to Maple Lane, located on the other side of the state.

It was on my way back to Maple Lane that I figured out I wanted my life to consist of traveling to vast regions of the world. I still don't know what the exact purpose for the traveling would be, but I definitely wanted to help others get from one place to another.

My life is a reflection of the planet earth. I feel we are one and have experienced the same reality. Just as I went through a spell of dark years, the planet derailed and re-surfaced through the unforgettable dark ages. And those dark times are needed in their reality because they define who you are as a person. In my beliefs, life sometimes calls upon you to define who you really are by demonstrating an aspect of who you are not. This I believe is why a portion of my life happened the way it did. Everything has a purpose and there is no such thing as accident or coincidence. You create your own reality by conscious and unconscious thought, therefore, if you don't believe you create your own reality you will experience something not of your creation proving that you "indeed" create your own reality. I think at some level I always knew this truth, but I just had to experience hot before I could really feel cold. Of course, I was taught the difference between dark and light, but knowing something and experiencing something are two different things. Your "True Self" knows everything, so then the purpose of life is not to learn, but to remember, create and experience - nothing more, nothing less.

I believe in my twenty years of existence, I've had my fair share of bad, or should I say, unique experiences. I am now on the right path to finding my true self, and I've managed to make it through the roughest part of my life, unless I haven't. You can't always tell the future, but you can mold the present into the reality you want to experience for the future. Nothing has meaning at all until you give it meaning. So the real question is, have you given yourself meaning lately? If not, you mean nothing at all. Start with the self and work from there.

Epilogue

It is now September 2G and four months has elapsed from when I had originally finished this project, but I decided to put down a finishing touch just to show the readers how unpredictable life is and will continue to be. With great thanks to my father I was able to go on one last trip to visit my mother in Spokane before she made her transaction to the spirit world on the 13th of June '00.

While on the visit in Spokane, I sat next to my mom gripping her hand and talking to her while she lay comatose in bed. Her only movement was slight twitching of the fingers and occasional spasmodic motion of the muscles above her eyes. I read to her a little bit out of a book she had read shortly before slipping into a comma, ironically titled, *The Tibetan Book of Living and Dying*. I felt she was well prepared to die and even though she loved my sister and me dearly, there was no holding on. The time had come and we all knew it. I just wished I could have given her a hug, but at the time I was incapable to perform such a task due to the chain strapped tightly around my waist from which my wrists were hooked to, restricting my arm movement to minimum. I settled for a kiss on the forehead before I left, making my long trek which voyaged across the entire state of Washington. I was sort of in a hypnotic state while driving back, knowing that this would be the last time I would see my mother on the physical plane. It seemed as though I was in an Alice-in-Wonderland world, in which things did not seem as they appeared. I was at a complete loss. However, I quickly grasped the closed circle and came to the realization that this experience will only strengthen my life energy in the long run and so, to let go and accept would be the most beneficial thing for me to do. And so I did. And when the news came five days later that my mom had passed, I accepted it as though someone had told me what the weather forecast for the day was. As though it was an every day occurrence and indeed, it is.

Death, I believe, is just another stage in life, an important stage, and when you truly know this it will reduce your sense of loss into the smallest grain of sand which will spontaneously manifest itself into the seed of life, and depending on your faith and mind state, will grow into an unending flow of joy like that of a river finding its way to a waterfall. And as the water falls, it is set free by the free fall of realization. And so I realized that death was nothing more than life taking on a different form. For life proceeds everything, it is the all-in-all. And I remembered, that is, I re-membered my mom's golden rule of survival into my life: Love is all there is.

Shortly after my mom's transaction, I was informed by my dad that I had a brother. At first thought, I assumed he meant that my step-mom Mia, who I've known for almost 10 years, was pregnant.

I quickly second guessed asking, "What do you mean? How is this?"

"Well," my dad started, "a while back, after I left Spokane, I had a couple of casual relationships that never really amounted to anything, or so I thought. Next thing I know, I getta' call."

To me, this just didn't seem to be - real. You only saw this sort of thing happen while watching Date Line or Jerry Springer on TV. My brain seemed to be spinning like the rollers inside of a VCR while on fast forward. Numerous questions were flying through my head all at once and I finally responded as casually as I could.

"How do you know its yours? I mean, your son?"

"Oh, we ran some blood tests and the results came back positive," my dad said, as if he was explaining what he had eaten for lunch earlier that day.

"Annd," I asked, "they wanted to prove you were the father because?"

"So they could get the child support money that they never got," my dad stated.

"How much money did they get?" I asked knowing it would probably be a lot.

"Ahh, roughly around the neighborhood of 20K," my dad choked out.

"20G's," I exclaimed, "Damn, that hurts."

"Yep, right out of the pocket book. There one minute and gone the next," my dad sighed.

"Doesn't that make you kinda' mad," I said in a straight to the point tone.

"Well, I mean, ya' gotta' understand, they're in the right and so the money should legally go to him, but yeah, it is a little frustrating. It's not something you really expect," my dad explained in mild calmness.

And I'll admit, it was very much unexpected, which I sometimes think should be the definition of life when you look it up in the dictionary. Even though one of my main mottoes in life is "expect the unexpectable" it still came to me as a moderate shock. Not really a bad one, just a damn-I-didn't-know-that.

The rest of the conversation over the phone consisted of more questions from me. All I know to this day is that my brother's (half brother's) name is Chris, he's mulatto like myself, he's around 18 or 19 years old and lives in the Tri-Cities area, located in southeast WA. My sister's reaction was about the same as mine. I asked her if she was going to go meet him, and she told me that she would probably try to get a hold of him on the phone before she went traveling to the Tri-Cities. I told her that I definitely wanted to meet him, but that I just hoped he wasn't a square. To tell the truth, I always kind of wanted a brother in my earlier days of growing up and I guess I got my wish — it was just kind of late. And if that doesn't prove that thought can be made manifest then I guess the statement itself must be false. But as it is, I believe it to be truth, for that's the conclusion I've come to while putting my life on paper and reviewing it. Although thought may be a slow method of creation, it never the less creates tangible outcomes.

There comes a time when you think you may have a fix on life, but in actuality life has a fix on you. In truth you and life are one, but life represents your True Being, your Total Self; the higher consciousness of yourself that already knows everything about everything and so it is the entity of yourself, which can be defined as life, that controls every outer set of circumstances you experience. This is the divine dichotomy, in which both realities take place at the same time, conflicting and comforting the other. In a sense you create everything that you experience, but it is in a higher sense that everything proceeds out of life which is the ultimate creator, and so it is only when you look closely at this, or rather, come to realize that both senses are possible and are indeed, happening at the same time because they are, of course, one. The point I am trying to make here, and through this entire chapter of my life, is that life is just a big contradiction in which you can never know what lies beyond the next corner of your future, but at the same time you create every second of it in the ever lasting eternal moment of now. You create it, yet it creates you, and so the process will never end, for it is not bound by time. It is endless and has never not been. It, life, is a process of immaculate and utter simplicity. It is a process. Life.

LIFE STRUGGLES

CHANG SAECHAO

When I was almost 7 years old, my parents told us the news that we would be moving to America. That was my parents' dream - to bring us into a better world. The news wasn't something we took lightly. We were all dreaming for a better world, to be "where money grows on trees."

Childhood, Part I

The first day of my life started when my mom gave birth to me. When I was growing up, I was happy. As my mom recalls it, she said that I was a good boy growing up. I don't know how much I weighed, but I know that I was a chubby little kid. I was born in 1982, in Thailand, East Asia. My name is Chang Saechao. The second year of my life was scary because my sister was babysitting me. I crawled a lot so my sister didn't really pay any attention to me, so I crawled and dropped into our water well. My sister heard the splash of the water. She came running and looked into the well and saw me floating. (I never recall this, but my father told me). By then my parents were coming home. My dad heard my sister screaming and ran over to see what it was about. Then he saw me floating. He jumped down the well and got me out. But I was a baby and hardly breathing. My stomach was all bloated up, and my dad put me over his shoulder and pushed my back. The water rushed out of my stomach and I lived to watch another day and year go by.

When I was three I don't really recall anything but dogs barking and licking my face. Then I was four. I recall a lot of things from there because I was about that age when my parents got a horse. I don't recall the name my parents gave him, but I rode the horse all the time. I couldn't walk far, so me and my little brother always rode the horse.

Then, when I hit age 5, I was starting to love Thailand. It was a beautiful country. Thailand was nothing but green and fields of rice and animals. I was always going someplace I know that wasn't too dangerous. I remember that I always fished, I loved to do outdoor stuff. I'd love to play with knife and axe. I love chopping down trees, and hunting for honey. The way you get honey is that you have to find the beehive first, then you have to chop down the tree. The process was painstaking and hard work. After the tree is chopped down you run for dear life, the bees are about 1.5 inches and all black. The bees are almost like the "bumble" bees. If you ever seen a big "bumble" bee, just add two of them together and you get a bee that looks like the ones we have in Thailand. After the tree is chopped and you run, you go back with a branch of dead wood and leaves. You have to light the branch and smoke the bees out. You have to get the bees drunk. Then you have to chop the opening of the beehive. Then you get a basket and you have honey.

Then, when I hit the age of 6, I was running around crazy, looking for what I could chop down. While I was chopping down the tree, I accidentally placed my hand in the wrong place and chopped my pinky finger on my left hand. The finger I chopped was lacerated. I went home, not really crying but in shock, cause I split my finger in half. The finger was bleeding profusely. When I got home, my mom freaked out and started screaming, not really helping me out. I just got a roll of cloth and wrapped it around my finger. Then my mom stopped screaming and looked at my finger. My mom went out and got this plant that she chewed and put on my finger and re-wrapped the cloth around my finger. The plant that she used took the pain and numbness there on my finger, then my whole hand went numb.

A month later, I went out again and started doing what I love the most, chopping down trees for firewood. I don't really know why I'm not scared cause I had just chopped my finger. I guess I'm never scared of anything, because if you love to do something you just keep on doing it. The thing I liked doing most is shooting birds or anything that can be killed by a "slingshot." I would usually take the two dogs that I used to hunt with. The two dogs' names were Yellow and Red cause one of them had a yellowish tint to it and the other, a reddish tint. I remember the first thing that I killed was a Red Squirrel. I shot it and it fell into the river and the dogs would swim and get the squirrel I killed. The only way you could kill a squirrel with a "slingshot" is to shoot it in the head. Any other body part you hit wouldn't do anything because the rock would just bounce off the soft parts of its body. One day my two brothers went hunting. One of the guns they used backfired on my oldest brother, burning his face all black.

When I was almost 7 years old, my parents told us the news that we would be moving to America. That was my parents' dream - to bring us into a better world. The news wasn't something we took lightly. We were all dreaming for a better world to be in, "where money grows on trees." That line was used so many times as we were coming to America. The last few months we sold our animals. Our horse which was called Red, was the biggest horse I ever seen, standing about 17 hands tall. I didn't want to sell the horse, but we were going to America so it must be done. The horse was sold to this "Laos" people. I never knew how much the horse was sold for. Then came our dogs which I didn't want to leave behind but had to. We gave them to our cousins to take care of.

Then came the rice fields. We had to give that to our friends and relatives. We sold most of our rice and the house we sold too. Everything we had that was worth something was sold because we couldn't bring them with us. My dad was a very skilled hunter that had a lot of guns and cross bows that were all sold and got some money. We needed the money to purchase clothing so we would have something new to wear when we reached the new land that was rich. I remember hearing them talk about it. To me, I was very scared because of the new land, I don't have friends in America and all the things I know were of my home land, not the new world. I was so scared that I ran away to my cousin's house and stayed there until my parents came and got me.

We had two more months before we were to move to another place to live and have our name called. The last two months were nothing but sadness for me because of the things that were on my mind. I was always thinking, what's going to happen when we leave this place? I turned the sadness into a little happiness by going fishing and looking for honey. One month before we were due at the camp, my parents had a party to celebrate us going to America and being rich. As time came close to us leaving, I got scared and harder on my sadness. The sadness came down to depression which caused me to become very skinny. I did not eat and my parents were getting very worried. The depression became hard for that month, it was so bad that somehow my ears got very infected. My parents took me to the city and they did all these tests on my ears and gave me so many shots on my butt that it left a scar there till this day. The shots kept on repeating and the shots they gave me wasn't helping at all. It made matters worse by giving me so many shots. I became sick and couldn't move for days. If somebody were to speak loud to me, my ears would start ringing because it was so sensitive. Then time came for us to get to the camp that we were supposed to live in until they called our names, and then we would live in another camp.

Leaving the house and everything behind was hard on my parents because they were the only two people that built the house, and my dad and mom were the ones to field the rice and the ones to fertilize the soil. They were the only two people that cried when we left. (Till this day, I can't believe that my parents were the ones that built it, everything from nothing.) The drive to the camp was hard because the "lorry" truck was hard on the roads. There were no roads that were made to travel on so the long hours riding the "lorry" was a gruesome experience. The ride was very long. They would stop at every home and we would have our bathroom breaks. Then the truck would go on, and we would hop on and ride for a couple of hours. The people I feel sorry for were the people riding on top of the lorry truck. They had no seat and the hood was very hard on your butt. Then the other hard thing was the bugs that would bite and suck blood or some would just sting you for fun. My brother got stung so bad that he was itching all over, and his face was nothing but red bumps and his eyes were puffed up. He couldn't even really see anything so him and my other brother (Nai) changed spots and my brother (Nai) got smart and wore a sweater to cover his head and a bandanna for his face. As the ride went by we saw light, then everybody cheered because they were all happy to stand on ground and get up from their butts so the numbness would go away.

The camps were nothing but long houses that were separated by a wall. The rooms were nothing really big like the house we had, but they had to do because we would stay until they call our names. The camp was not big and there were about 5 or 6 long houses. By the camp there was a dam and a bridge. I had never seen anything like it so I just looked on and on until my mom called me. The bridge was a very interesting sight, another sight were cars. I'd never seen a car till then, and I became very interested in it. The first day at the camp was very hard for me because there weren't any animal noises around or surrounding the place. I couldn't sleep, and my ears were still infected. As days went by there was nothing to do but wait until our family name was called.

When our name was called, these people called "Mong," they took pictures for us and got our social security number to give to us and give us the birthcard and other things so we could pass and go to another camp. That is where we come to America. As days pass by the temperature rises and becomes very humid.

People started dying because of the weather and there weren't any doctors close by so death came and kept on taking life as another day passes.

The days just kept on going, and I started to go to the dam and fish. At first I couldn't catch anything because I didn't know what kind of fish "lurk" in the water so I just kept using worms and a hook. I kept on going back and catching nothing. I started getting very frustrated of catching nothing. One day I was done finishing up and going back to the house, but there came a kid about my age with fishing gear. He stopped and looked at me and said - You're not going to catch anything when you pick up your line every ten minutes. I said - Like you could do any better. Then he said that he could and he'll show me. He said that the only fish that lived in the water is catfish. Which only bite at nighttime. He said just put your line over night and come back the next morning and pull it out. I did what he told me and left it over night. The next morning I was so pumped and amped that I ran to the lake and pulled the line out. The first thing that came to my mind when the line became heavy was that I got nothing but seaweed. I was very disappointed because I thought I didn't catch anything, but then I started pulling it harder and felt the line start wiggling, and I knew then that I caught something big. As the line came in, I saw the ugly catfish. I thought - Can that ugly thing be edible?

Catfish has these stingers on their fins and back fins. I knew nothing of that and when I started taking the hook out of its mouth, it stung the hell out of me. I pulled my hand back and looked at the palm and saw a trickle of blood. The pain started intensifying and I started cursing. Hell and heaven wouldn't want to hear it coming from English or my native tongue. I knew then how to take the hook out. The way you do it is, when you pick up the fish, you have to hold it on the head and palm it down its back slowly, so that its fins don't pop out and sting you. As I got the hook out of the fish mouth, I then wormed the hook and tossed it back in the water. Then I took the big catfish back to my mom.

The moment I got back home and my mom saw the fish she ran to me and took the fish. I followed her to the living room. When I came in and my mom saw me, she said good job for catching the fish. Then she told me that we don't have that much food left, that the catfish will do us good for the time being. I looked into my mom's eyes and said I could get more fish and I still have my slingshot with me. When I woke up and ran to get my lines I didn't know that my brothers and sister were gone, so was my dad. I asked my mom where they went. She told me that they have to work from dawn till dusk. My mom told me they work like slaves for the "mong" people. We have to work for our share of the food. I wanted to work, but my mom said that I was too young. Then she said I was her champion because I got the fish. Then she told me to go play. I told her that I was going hunting, and she said be careful.

I went into the world with my slingshot and rocks that are very round and could go through the air without problems. The morning was good, and there was plenty of things I could kill. The only things I really saw were birds that were very small so I didn't want to kill them when I can't use them. I started going in further to the woods. As I went into the woods, I saw squirrels and rabbits. I took a rock and put it in the leather pouch and pulled back, aimed, and let loose. It hit the squirrel right on the head and killed him or knocked him out until I got close enough and knocked him over the head with a stick. By then the rabbit ran to the nearest rock to hide. I saw it and tricked him to come out, by standing very still and not moving. It seems I stand there for a couple of minutes, and he came out. When he came out I saw that I couldn't get a clear shot in the head, so the choice I had was to go for the hind leg. So when it hit, he can't run too fast. By then I would have to reload and kill. I took aim and let go and wap. I heard something snap and seen the rabbit try to run but couldn't go anywhere. So I ended his life with another shot. I picked up the rabbit and started heading back home but saw something move in the tree. I then saw what it was. It was a bird, but not a bird, what we call in our language a "chicken bird." The bird looks like a chicken that flies, and it's pretty big. I knew that if I didn't hit that "chicken bird" on the head I would have no chance in killing him. Then I thought about what my oldest brother taught me - when you hit something on the chest and if you break the ribs you would kill it. I knew that then I could kill the "chicken bird." I took aim and shot the bird on the chest. I saw the poof of feathers and saw the bird falling from where it nested. I ran over and shot it another time in the head. Then I picked up the animals that I'd killed and went back home.

Then it was almost dinner time. When I got home, I saw my mom. I smiled and lifted up the things I killed. She came running at me and started doing the same thing as when I got the fish. I went into the kitchen with my mom. She gave me a bucket to fill with water and to boil so she could pluck the feathers and fur the animals.

I got the bucket and went down to the lake, got a bucket of water. I then saw the little boy that helped me catch the fish. I asked where he lived. He said that he lived a couple of blocks from where we lived. I asked him if he wanted to come over to my house so we could play. He said that he would, if he gets permission from his mother.

About two months went by before our name was called. We got all the things we needed to pass. They said that we have three days to get ready and the "lorry" will come and pick us up with the other members of the family. When I found out that "Kao" was the other family that would ride with us I became very happy because him and I are very good friends. The day the "lorry" came and picked us up we were very happy to be moving to another camp which was the last refugee camp we had to stay. The ride was to be for two days because we had to cross the border between Thailand and Cambodia so we could reach the camp. Then from there to America.

The ride was even harder this time because the roads were unknown and not very many people traveled on them. The dangerous road was nothing but death and rocks so traveling was very hard for the old and young ones, one which was my little brother who was only 5 years of age. His name is "Lai." He would always cry and he would throw up the food he would eat. The ride was stopped and we set camp with tents, and we would wake up and leave very early in the morning because of the Cambodia soldiers attacking us. My mom took us to the tents and started fixing dinner, and we were all hungry.

She was fixing something that smelled good, which were rabbits, squirrels, birds, frogs, and big rats, which I trap with "bamboo" snapper. My dad taught me the trap. So the dinner got done, my dad gathered all the kids and other people around to tell us the story where he hunted the biggest deer he ever seen, I had heard the story already but was very fascinated to hear my dad telling it.

The next day when everybody was aboard the lorry, the travel began again with numb butts and bug bites. As the hours went by it started to get dark, and out of nowhere there were soldiers standing out and pointing guns on the drivers. These were the border controllers. The border controller took all our things and went through them. They took my slingshot, and I almost cried because that was the only thing I had that would hold memories for me. They then started counting the people. The border controller took us to a prison saying that we had to spend ten days in it so that everything would be clear. They locked all the families that were supposed to come to America in the little room. The first day in the refugee camp prison wasn't so nice, because there were rats in that place crawling around, chewing our belongings. They didn't feed us, so everybody went hungry. People started crying like the little ones. The adults were taken to the fields and worked till dusk.

For me, being in the prison wasn't so nice because I was never held or detained in a place. I would have bad dreams and wake up crying in the day time. I was scared of them taking my mom away. I would be alone, and have nobody to care for me. I would hug my mom tight when she would walk about, talking to people. She would pick me up and we would go everywhere together.

One day I had a dream so bad that I woke everybody in the prison. The dream was that I lost both my parents. I woke up crying and my mom rushed towards me and hugged me. She started crying saying - My baby, don't cry. She said she can't take this no more, that I would wake up screaming, having bad dreams. My dad would calm us both down until I would sleep on my mom's arm, and she would sleep on my dad's arm.

The second day my dad gathered all the other families and put the money together to see if that would get us out of prison. The money all came to about 60,000 bat which in American money would be about $15,000. My dad talked to the guard and the guard talked to the guy who was running the place. The guy came, and they talked for hours. Then, finally, my dad came and told everybody to pack their bags and that we were free to go. As we packed, I felt very happy that I would go with my mom. When the packing of all the families was done, we were led into the lorry and then the next destination was the last camp. Then we would come to America. This time the camp was more livable. The house was clean and it was bigger. There was plenty of food because this time the food was given to you. The days went by quick. The next thing I knew was that we would hop on the plane, and America, here we come.

Our name was called and the next morning we were heading toward a big plane which my dad said was a 747. Before we got on the plane, they showed us a video of America which was nice. It had a lot of big buildings, and the most beautiful homes I'd ever seen. The only thing they didn't show was the bums and hobos (which means homeless people). The tape left the people who were poor out of the picture. I know now that America was selling false information to people. I never knew why they did that, but they shouldn't do anything like that. For me, I expected the US to be the richest place you ever been to, not to walk around downtown Seattle and see all the homeless. That made me mad cause the video showed all the rich places and not the other side of poverty. To me, if I was to show people of my country, I'd show them. When I came to America and seen this place, I wanted to go back to my old land, my country. You don't have to be homeless if you are poor, you just go into the jungle and make what you got. That's the good thing about my country.

The other things the Americans didn't show is racism. I was a child thinking America is going to be a nice place to live. When I got here and white people was the, well, like "race" in America. That was not the fairest thing for a child to think about. Why is there such a thing call racism in America? To me, if you are racist you have no life. Why do you hate people that are not the same color as you are? If you hate other races cause their skin colors are not the same. The fact is that I think you don't like them cause maybe the other race work harder than you. You find that hard to believe, that they work harder than you. Plus this was once all your country. Now things have changed, and the white man don't like that, so they cause problems for colors, like the KKK (Ku Klux Klan). They decide that white people are the number one race in the world. Well, sorry to tell you this, but the facts are changing. A statistic says by the year 2085 there won't be anything called white cause everyone will be mixed.

After the video we started moving onto the planes. The plane, which was very big, looked like a tin can. I asked myself, how is this thing going to fly?

Childhood, Part II

The plane that we went on was so big that I thought that I was in a house. The wait to take off was getting very long. The thought of my flying in a plane was a very gruesome experience. I was very scared of flying. I asked myself -What if the plane went down? I would just want to sit with my mom. My mom only told me to go back to my seat and she would give me "bubble gum," which in America was called Bazooka, which in my homeland was much thicker and sweeter. Then I would just chew my boredom out of my mind. As we waited, the flight attendant told us to buckle our seat belt, which I had no clue which way to do it. Plus- we don't know one word of English. We had an interpreter for us that knew a little English to get us by. When the plane started the engine, it made this really noisy sound. I jumped up on my seat and thought that the plane was about to blow up. Then my mom said that everything was all right. I then just sat and waited until the plane got to the runway. The plane started out fast and got faster. The noise was so loud now that my ears were starting to ring and I was getting a big headache.

Then the nose of the plane started going upward which rushed the blood all the way back to my toes. The tingles started in my stomach and then rushed up to my chest, and it felt like a roller coaster ride. The sensation was the first thing I ever felt that felt good and scary at the same time. The plane started its way up into the blue sky.

When I was about five, I wonder how it would feel to be close, so close to the sky and touch the cloud and feel the cool breeze, but some of the fantasy would happen and some of it wouldn't. But it felt good just to see the sky. As the plane climbed upward toward the blue sky, I felt light-headed and the tingly feeling started coming at me again. Then the plane stopped climbing and leveled out and the loud noise started going down. Then when the plane became smooth on the air and the ride was smoother and the sky was bluer. As the ride dragged on, my head got lighter and lighter and I started getting very dizzy and felt like vomiting in the plane. I didn't know where I could vomit at but asked my mom. My mom told me to go to the bathroom, which I didn't know. Then the person interpreting for us told me how to use the bathroom. I then ran towards the bathroom, holding my mouth so that nothing would come out before I reached the toilet bowl.

The plane went on for hours and I kept on getting light headaches. And for every hour I kept on going to the toilet bowl. The vomiting kept on coming until I ran out of things to come out of my stomach. As the plane went on and on, then the seat belt light came on and I had to buckle my belt. The flight attendant came out and said that we were about to land. As the plane touched the ground, the plane made a big jolt, and I almost screamed. Then it made this crack sound. Then the engine noise came back again.

The plane was gliding through the land nicely and my thoughts and sense of feeling came back. The plane started slowing down and a the big thing came beside the door. The door opened up and we climbed out of the plane. The interpreter helped us out and told us to get our things and wait. The wait seemed to go on and on because there was nothing to do, and we had no money to buy food. The place where we waited was somewhere in Africa. The wait seemed to take forever. Because it started getting dark. Then our plane was ready from fueling up and we took off on the plane again. The whole trip took up about 18-24 hours because of the waiting and the fueling of the plane.

The plane took off, the flight attendant said that our next stop would be in America, our new homeland. As the plane climbed and climbed, my sense of feeling went away, because every time I looked out the little window I saw little cars, houses, and nothing but oceans of water. The second trip wasn't too gruesome because I got a little bit used to the plane, and I had nothing in my stomach so there was nothing to worry about. But I was wrong. I soon started to get light headed again, and this time when there was nothing to come out, it was worse.

As the hours dragged by the plane was moving a little bit faster. Then the flight attendant said, that we were to put on our seat belts because we to land soon. As the pointy nose dropped I felt very scared. The plane might crash and you'll never know. The plane made the same motion jolt as before when it hit the ground with the force.

When the plane landed, we came out of the plane. My dad's side of the family stood there waiting for us. They hugged us and we hugged them back. They took us out and went to their van which was a gray Toyota which was very nice looking. They drove us to their own apartment which was full with "Asians." The apartment complex was very weird looking because it was very dirty looking and was not too big and not too small. Which left us in the middle sized apartment.

They took us up the stairs and led us into room 308. Until this day I will remember that place. There were two bedrooms in the place and everything we needed to start a new life. We had cable TV, a stove, and everything we needed. The apartment was rented for us by my grandfather. They said within 2 months my parents would have to look for jobs. For me, this place was strange and lonely looking. The air didn't smell too good, and there was lots of noise coming from the streets, and you could hear the loud thumping of "American music."

I didn't understand any of these things, but I will learn from it. The year we came to America was 1989 which was around June so it was the summer there. There was no school at that point, which was good for me. As the days went by, both my parents found jobs at Thai restaurants. They would work a lot just to get the things we needed like mattresses, pans, clothing, food, and the apartment rent. We didn't have to pay for water or garbage.

Then the days flew by. I never got used to America, because the surroundings were so different. I never made any friends which I think was because of my attitude towards other kids. They spoke English and I didn't. But my life was changed and so were my surroundings and my attitude would have to change, too. So I started talking with other kids. The first friend I had was named Chang like my first name, but we called him Julie, which was a girl's name but it fit him. The next friend was named BJ which I never knew his real name but they called him BJ, so did I. The English language was never hard for me so I picked up a lot of words that were mostly bad like fuck, mother fucker, and other things. But I knew English words so I started using them. Then it reached September and I had to go to school. I didn't feel too good about it but I had to go.

On September 9th, I got ready to go to school with my Jansport backpack and new clothing. I had to walk to the bus stop and my friends would help me get to the bus stop and they would just leave me. That day I didn't go to school because I was so scared of the white kids and other kids. So I went home and my mom found me. I got my butt beat, so next time it would be harder. The next day I went to school. As I waited at the bus stop, I would see other kids, but they would never come close to me. They went into other buses, so I waited for mine. The bus number was 522 which came around 7am. Then I saw the big yellow bus. The bus stopped and the door opened with a swoops sound, and I jumped back. Then I looked at the bus driver, it was a big black woman. Then she said with the sound of almost a man, "Are you coming in or not?" I just jumped in the bus and went back to the seat and waited. As the bus made its rounds other kids started filling up the bus. The noise got louder and other kids started looking funny and giving me the eyes and then rolled them back in their heads. I didn't pay any attention to them. My mom told me that we're different from other kids who were white. She said when they look at you don't pay attention to them, be strong and don't get into trouble. The bus that was taking us to school was loud and noisy. No other kid sat by me, and I was the only color on the bus except the bus driver.

The bus took us to Lawten elementary school. The school was nothing but white people, or most of them. I was the second Asian in there. I forgot to mention that my friend BJ's sister was at that same school. She rode the same bus with me. The school was big and clean looking. The roof was blue and the walls were made from red brick which were very new looking. The lunchroom was big and had big tables. I went there for breakfast. They called me to the office after I ate breakfast which was cold cereal. They asked me why I wasn't at school yesterday. I told them why and then I was on my way to English class. The school teacher's name was Mrs. Hamburger. She was an old woman. I really don't know much about her. She was like a teacher. The first grade wasn't too bad until I was getting picked on by white kids. I don't know why they picked on me until they started calling me a "gook," which I didn't know what it meant until I asked my teacher, and she said it was a racial slur toward Asians. Then I started getting mad at white people and hated them till this day.

The second grade was the same thing, getting picked on and

getting into fights with white kids. How did I feel when I got picked on? I really don't know. At first, when this kid said that I couldn't sit at the table and you can't stand at the front of the line and you can't play with us. I said okay. But as time went on and second became third grade, the "picking" never stopped. Then I had thoughts. Why are they picking on me? I never knew why they picked on me. They said it was the color of my skin. But aren't we all human? Till this day, I never knew why they picked on me. The teachers never knew about it because the kids never picked on me when I was around them. So I stayed by the teachers most of the time. I never played with the other kids. I just kept everything to myself. I never questioned anybody. So that was my world when I was picked on. I never told my parents because they were never home. They worked all the time, so I never knew who to trust.

At fourth grade, I started skipping school. I would wait until 8:45 after the bus dropped us off. I then would go to the bathroom and wait until 9:15. I would then walk out of the bathroom, walk outside. I couldn't walk 50 miles, so I would steal a bike every time I skipped school. My parents never knew because they would work late and come home and go to bed. That was their Monday through Friday. I never told them what happened. They wouldn't understand the problems facing me. That's what I thought when I was young.

The fifth grade, that's when the teachers started knowing that I was hardly at school. They would sometimes call me into the office and talk to me but I never talked to them because it was an all white school. So they would let me go to the "hell" class - that's what I called school. Skipping school was fun because sometimes I would go to the K mart and steal this fishing pole that was very short and then you pull it out, like a TV antennae. I would put it in my backpack with all the other stuff to go with the fishing pole and skip school. Then go to the docks of Puget Sound and catch salmon.

One day I was going to do it again, and I waited until 9:15 and walked out. As I was walking, I was spotted by a teacher. I didn't know until it was too late. I was walking and suddenly a white car pulled up and a big black man got out of the car and took me back to school. When they took me back to the office, they emptied out the contents of my backpack. What they saw surprised them, because their eyes got big and their mouths dropped open. The principal took me into the office and started talking to me. I escaped to the world where nobody could hear me and I couldn't hear them. Soon he got tired and stopped talking to me and let me go back to class.

One day the principal took me into his office and started asking these weird questions like - Are your parents aware of what you're doing? And do they know you're acting this way? Are they beating you? And so on. I told them no and mind your own business. At home my parents and siblings didn't know I was going through these things. To me, it was me against the world.

Two months before the school year was supposed to end, the whole fifth grade was supposed to attend a camping trip. I wasn't planning on going because I knew that I was going to get picked on. I got all the things I needed to attend the camping trip, but I wasn't going. I did all that because I didn't want my parents nagging on me about the trip. But the school had other things on their mind. They would have me going on the trip. So I didn't have any way out of it. So I went along with all the fifth graders in the school.

The name of the camp was called Camp Polcayla. The camp was located around the ocean. I don't know where, but it was on an island in the middle of nowhere. The trip to camp was 6 hours long, and we would be gone for 3 days without parents or anybody else but teachers and cooks for the camp.

When I got to school, the teachers took me and never let me out of their sight. Then around 12:30 after everyone had lunch, the bus came and was waiting to take us to camp or the docks to the ferries. We would have to ride the ferry for four hours when we got to the docks. As we all got into the two buses, we waited until the head count was all checked, and then the bus started moving. The bus ride took 1 and a half hours long.

The bus ride was boring and loud. I was the only Asian in that bus and the whole camping trip was white. So I sat all the way in the back of the bus so I wouldn't get picked on. The bus ride was getting to me, so I opened the window and let some fresh air in. As the bus ride took us I started feeling lonely because nobody talked to me, and I had no friends in the whole school. So I sat back and let the loneliness take me to the pain in my heart. I always thought that I would never have friends. That hurt me very deep as a kid growing up. Having no friends was not that fun because I never got to do anything that was fun. I never was social with other kids. I would think that I wasn't liked because I never talked to the other kids. I then came up with a good thought that I would be friends with some people when we reached the camp.

When the ride was over we had reached our destination, the docks for the ferries. The wait was about thirty minutes. The docking had all kinds of goodies but I barely had anymore money, so I didn't bother with snacks. I was the only one sitting on the corner doing nothing but watching other kids eat the snacks from the vending machines. I could outlast hunger for a very long time, so I wasn't worried about food.

The ferry arrived and the passengers, which was us, went onto the big boat. The ride would take us four hours and the camp people would wait with buses and other cars to come and pick us up. The ferry ride was very interesting because I had never been on one, so the gruesome experience was nice. I would ride by myself which was in the back of the ferry with a little porch thing. And I would just sit there. I sat there for the whole ride.

When I sat alone I had a very nice time. The ocean breeze was nice, the wind felt good on my skin, my hair would flop around on my head. The cold was starting to get to me because I didn't bring a coat with me. After three hours I was freezing, but I didn't care as long as I'm out there no one would come and pick on me. Plus, I really didn't want to be around other kids.

When we reached our destination, Camp Polcayla, we all packed our things and walked out of the ferry. As I suspected, the buses were waiting for us. We all climbed in the bus and waited. As the bus started moving, a kid wanted to sit by me so I let him. The kid, who was white, started talking to me and then all of a sudden he started talking shit, saying Asians were nothing but losers and we were good for nothing. Then he got up and walked back to his friends. And then I heard him say, "I'll never back down from a dare."

I felt used and sad because why would the kids' parents teach them those things. I wanted to cry so hard but I couldn't because my heart didn't feel like crying and that hurt because I had never done "the hating of race" to anyone. The hate came to me, then the plan getting to know other kids wouldn't work. So I kissed it good-bye. Sometimes I would think of suicide. I would come close but never do it. And I felt like doing it right there. To be picked on is not a light thing. People might say they got picked on while they were little, but nobody has been in the same shoes as me. The pain I felt came from the heart. Physically the pain wasn't great, but emotionally it was other things. I really couldn't do nothing but feel the pain going through my heart, so I would sit back and "enjoy the pain."

When the bus ride was over, we got out. They said that we were to wait for instructions, then the teacher started calling our names for the cottage we were supposed to go to. The cabin was one big room with bunk beds. It would fit 11 people. The bunk beds were stacked on top of each other, 2 on the right, the other 2 on the left. The other kids set out and unpacked.

The first day of the camp was not fun because I never went out except to eat the three meal thing. The second day was the same thing - just chillin in my room, I didn't want to talk to anyone because it always hurt my emotional feelings. When that happens you don't feel nothing but pain.

The third day this girl named Emily came and started wandering around the cottage I was in. She never picked on me, so I went out and said, what's up to her. She said that she was lost. So I talked to her and told her how to find her way back. She said that she was scared to walk back alone because it was almost dark outside. So I thought - what the hell?

She and I started walking. We came upon a place that's like an archway with dense bush around we had to walk through to get to her cottage. While we walked in, she came behind me and gave a heavy push on my back. I fell through the bush, and someone grabbed me. I started screaming. Then all I heard were giggles from other kids. They set me up. I got up, tears running down my cheek, ran back to my cottage, and stayed there till sun up when we would head back to the school and home for me. When the sun rose, the teacher gathered us up, and we sang some stupid song. I then got my things and waited till we left without speaking to anybody, without looking, too. The trip back was the same. The next day the school was ending. We all gathered outside and sang an old song called Make New Friends. I never knew how the chorus went so I didn't sing. Then school was out, and I went to middle school.

Teenage Incarceration, Part III

Home was still the same. I was about 11 years old now. I went to a middle school called Hamilton Middle School. The first day we had homeroom. We all met in the lunchroom and students were called out to pick up schedules. The school was mostly colors. I thought that was best for me because I didn't like white people then.

As the day went by, I started skipping with friends I made which were all Asian. My parents didn't really care, so I skipped some more and got into trouble with other kids at school. I would get into fights once a day just to get a kick out of it. Mostly the people we beat up were Asians. I never fought a white person because I might go too far and kill them because of the hate I had for them building up.

Days then months passed by before school was to end. The teacher called me up to the office and said that I was to pass all the grades and skip to the eighth grade. I got really happy then cause they said I was to graduate that same year when school was to end.

Before school was to end, I got kicked out because I had a blade in my locker and somebody snitched me off. So I got kicked out but I was supposed to go to night school on September 9th to a nice white people high school. So I said Fuck, no. I aint going to repeat the same shit over.

When I didn't attend high school, I was into other things like being a gang member. I was in a gang called Young Dragon Society, known as the Golden Dragon from San Francisco. I got into guns but never into drugs.

The reason I joined a gang was for protection and love. My friends were there more for me than my family. I didn't care about how my life was but I cared for the fun had. The money was cool too, because if I ran out of money, I would go to San Francisco to make my money. Can't tell how, but can tell that protection was needed for the job.

When I hit the age 13, I was young and wild for action. I would fight anybody that says something to me or my friend. Being young I had so much fun until that day I was walking down the street. People on the other end of the block were yelling at me. I remember the people who were yelling at me and one of my close friends. I pulled out a .22 caliber and started shooting at the group of people. Somehow I got trigger happy and went too far. After the shooting me and my homeboy ran from the scene, but I was apprehended 5 blocks from the crime scene.

The cops took me downtown and started asking me questions. I told them everything how and what happened. They took my statement and took me to DYS (Detention Youth Services). I stayed there for 6 months to hear my decline hearing. I thought my life was over when I was looking at 13 years if I get declined on. My decline hearing was scheduled on January 26, 1997. The hearing came and found that I was too young so they couldn't decline me so I was looking at 7 years of sentencing. My sentencing was due on March 4, 1997. The day I got locked up was October 19, 1996. My sentence was 5 to 6 years because I pleaded guilty to all charges which were assault one with a deadly weapon and assault two with a deadly weapon. I was happy that they didn't decline on me, so I got sent up to a JRA (Juvenile Rehabilitation Administration).

When they sent me up I thought "Maple Lane School," which they called the institution, I thought that they were big people and that they would take my "manhood" - my asshole. I was scared to death. I was a small teenager weighing 135 lbs. and 5 foot 3, which was very short.

When I came upon Maple Lane, I thought they had me at the wrong place. The place was nice looking with Maple trees on both sides of the street coming down all the way to the Administration building. When I got to Maple Lane I was to be at the intake cottage which keeps us for thirty days to get ready for open campus. It was a maximum security - open campus was a minimum security. The intake cottage was a tight unit. You can't break rules, if you do, you spend 24 hours in your room with one hour out, so they call it 23 and one. Where you do 23 hours in your room and you get one hour out where you get shower and recreation. The thirty days went by quick. So on April 11th I was sent to another cottage which is a building that holds 24 kids. I was given my clothing and radio stuff. Then I was put into room 23.

The next day I went to school and learned a lot of new things. The months turned to years. I then went to a working cottage where you work as a cook aid or helper. The best place where you can work is the "stocking" where you get paid the most, which was $1.50 per hour not $5.50 or $6.50 like a regular job.

Now that I am writing this book about myself I hope someday people will use this and not teach young kids to hate other kids because they're not the same color as you are. It's now 2000, and in September, I will leave this place and be released to community at a group home, a second step to freedom. I could've prevented all this thing from happening to me if I would have just left that thing alone and walked away. Then I would still be a free man. If I had a choice and went back in time to change it, I would still do the thing I did because being locked up helped me a lot. I graduate from this school and am taking the college course called Gateways program. I am planning on being a doctor and getting my PhD. I would say getting locked up makes you learn a lot of things. And this is what I learned.

JUVENILE LIFE

JOHNATHAN SMITH

I'm a normal human being who made normal human being blunders. I'm telling you this because I want you to understand everyone makes mistakes. Some of you readers might be able to relate to what I'm saying and others won't. I advise you to kick back and enjoy this chance to view things from an encaged black youth's perspective.

Prologue

Ladies and gentlemen, welcome to my world. I suggest you take a seat and hear my presentation. My name is Johnathan Dowand Smith, I am 17 years old. I'm a black young man living in this world of stress, or should I say trying to maneuver through this complex maze we call life.

I'm a normal human being who made normal human being blunders. I'm telling you this because I want you to understand everyone makes mistakes. Have open ears to hear what I'm saying. Some of you readers might be able to relate to what I'm saying and others won't. I advise you to kick back and enjoy this chance to view things from an encaged black youth's perspective. Some of the things in this story might be considered "negative." This is only because my life was negative, or how I put it, hard. During this encounter with me, you'll acquire knowledge of why I did the things I did and how my incarceration changed my ways.

In this written expression you will have a better insight on what I've been through. During this enclosure to the world I have shed tears of pain, confusion, frustration, loneliness, and anything else you can think of! I still have some time to do, but I can use it to my advantage. I've had plenty of time to analyze my life, and thanks to my real family and friends, I've changed. I also thank those guys I use to hang around with.

The reason why I thank those so-called friends is by not writing me, they helped me see that they weren't any good for me. I also learned not to depend on anyone, besides Johnathan Dowand Smith. *Stand on my own two feet no matter what I go through.* I've had more than enough time to think about my life and situation to change.

I started out at an early age committing crimes. I didn't do anything major though. I use to steal candy from the neighborhood stores. The reasons why I believe I did these things is because it gave me a kind of rush to take something without buying it. After a while I kinda got addicted to it. I would steal candy for no reason whatsoever. I knew it was wrong, but I wasn't getting caught for it so I felt like - why should I buy it when I could just take it? I had this mentality for awhile, until I was caught.

I remember I was caught for stealing some candy, and since I was too young to go to jail they just walked me home in handcuffs. I was so embarrassed, because all my friends and neighbors had seen me in handcuffs. The officer told my grandma what happened, and she said that she would handle it. She asked me why I did it, and I told her, "Just because." She told me the importance in abiding by the law, and she wouldn't tell my parents. She said, "I'll leave that up to you!" Well, you can probably guess what I did. I measured out the situation and decided that it would be better if I told them. I was punished and this humbled me for awhile, but when I was around my friends again, I started back up.

From stealing candy my behavior worsened. As I got older stealing candy was little kid stuff. I started hanging around the wrong crowd. I started stealing bigger things, with more value. I had the same attitude that I had about the candy. *Why buy it if I can steal it?* My surrounding helped keep me in captivity. In the Bible it says "if you sit with the scornful then you are one of the scornful." This is what I was. I take responsibility for my actions, but my so-called friends weren't any help. Whenever I talk to these so called friends I tell them that they didn't let me down, they just showed their true colors.

Anyway, back to my story. I started committing crimes because I liked to have nice things. My parents provided for me, but I was ungrateful. I felt like if I stole clothes then I would always have nice things. After a while, I started getting caught and spent some time behind bars. My parents said all they could, but I was not ready to listen. I thought about the stealing issue and decided not to go that route. I was good for awhile, but still hung around the same people. When I carried dialogues with these people, I would tell them that I didn't want to steal anymore cause it's stupid, plus I was getting caught. My so-called friends just placed others' ideals upon my conscience.

I started taking others' property, because I wanted the money to buy clothes and just like the candy situation, I started to get addicted. To make a long story short, I continued this behavior until I came across my greatest opponent, Juvenile Rehabilitation Administration, JRA. In my life I came across institution time before, but it never did stick. Readers please remember that I'm not glorifying my past, I'm just giving you a quick background check, you feel me? That's pretty much my quick criminal history. I've done a lot of things in my youth that I can't really explain besides expressing the fact that I did what I did then because I felt there was no harm in it.

I believe there is a cause and effect chain reaction. To me everything happens for a reason, and I believe I needed a change and so did the man up above. I now look at my imprisonment as a learning experience. I needed a readjustment, or in better words, a timeout in my life. *Could have changed my ways but not these days.* I feel like God gave me a chance to better myself, so I sit and evaluate my current circumstances for hours in my enclosed chamber. What I am pondering on is who I really am. I recognize the acts I've been involved in are wrong. I'm not ashamed of these things because I've gained experience and knowledge from them.

I have put my family and friends through a lot of pain because of my actions. These thoughts race through my consciousness and eat the insides of me. I've grown to realize I cannot change the past but I can start a new future. This is why I display the changes and goals physically. I don't tell my family what I want to do, I do what I want to do, you feel me? I do not want to dwell in a cell for the rest of my life because of careless acts. I have goals that I will accomplish. I'm the only one that can hold myself down. I now understand the reasons for my incarceration. I have plans that I just simply can't let fold.

I know it's my job to influence my generation in a positive way. I've been where they could be headed and I can possibly help them decide differently. I'm still young, but I can help!

Growing up, I had a good family, but I believe it's better to receive feedback from your peers. It's easier to listen to someone that's your age trying to help than someone older telling you what to do and what not to do. Everyday I'm working on making myself a better person. I try to help my peers as much as possible because it's my duty.

I had a dilemma with my ego, and I felt like I had to be the top dog. Eventually that gets old. Being selfish comes back to you, and it doesn't feel good getting what's coming. Treat people how you like to be treated, life goes by a lot easier. At 17 years of age I've learned a lot and I'm thankful. I plan to give back as much as I can to everyone. I have a clear head full of dreams that I can fulfill if I put my mind to it. Thanks for having open ears to my testimony!

Maneuvering through a Complex Maze

From my recollection I was born in the city of Centiville, IL, East St. Louis. I dwelled there for 5 years before relocating to Tacoma, WA. I only hibernated there for a year before migrating back to Illinois. I stayed in Illinois for another year or two before moving to Tennessee. I don't really remember much other than our stay was only temporary. My family and I vacated back to Tacoma. I was informed that this was only to visit my grandma.

I still remember on the way there, our car broke down. It was hilarious. We were in Washington and only 30 minutes from our destination, which was my grandma's house. Her name is Elgelena Smith. The first time we came out here I had met her, but I only vaguely remembered her.

Truthfully, I don't recall much about my childhood until ages 8 or 9. My grandma came and rescued us. We lived with her only momentarily. We then moved into some apartments. I believe our stay there was also short (about a year). We then moved from the east side of Tacoma to the south.

6309 South 'I' Street. I still reminisce about that house. Big four bedroom house. It was white and blue. There was an attic and a very large basement. I share so many memories of this place with my family. I lived there for about 5 years. Growing up on 63rd St. as a child, I was wild. I went from quiet to the exact opposite.

I was raised in a God-fearing family that attended church, for the most part, every Sunday. By going to church I was naturally taught to do right. The church imposed strong feelings about living for God. I thought of this as being boring. I often fell into a deep sleep while attending church service. My whole family are Christians so I felt forced into this type of lifestyle. I veered away from this as soon as I felt old enough to speak my mind.

During elementary school I quickly gained a reputation for fighting. I enjoyed the excitement of being a detriment to others. I was repeatedly kicked out of school for some type of physical altercation. This behavior continued and worsened. Before I knew it I was the main attraction at school. My friends, or should I say so-called friends, anticipated me brawling. I preserved good grades even though I was constantly in trouble.

In elementary I had few of what we call girlfriends. We did the usual little kid stuff like call each other, give little kisses, and write love letters, nothing major though. My male friends and I would talk forever on 3-way phone lines and sneak over to girls' houses.

Styles. I always had the clothes that were in style. I tried to stay with whatever was considered cool. I also kept whatever hair style was in. My parents and I got along well and had a pretty strong relationship. I was just a little kid doing little kid stuff.

In middle school (my adolescent years) is where my life diverted from "positive to negative" or how I would put it, "easy to hard." I remember my first day in middle school. I was scared, because everyone looked way bigger than me. I felt like I was the bottom of the food chain.

I was scared. I had problems finding my classes and would walk around aimlessly because of fear. This is where I put on a mask that would slide on and off until the middle of my physical bondage (Maple Lane). Every time it slid on the force was stronger. For some reason I felt like I had to show to others that I wasn't a punk. It seemed like it was just me *standing helpless*.

I went to John S Middle School. People soon found out I was a fighter by the way I vocalized things. I played basketball and other sports and was over all the most athletic. I was a stand-out and it was obvious. I was attractive, funny, loud, and an athlete. I took advantage of my talents and often threw them in my peers' faces. I was frequently called conceited or self-centered. This behavior escalated as I grew up. I continued the pattern of being good for a while, then fighting or getting into some kind of conflict. This resulted in my receiving time out of school a lot of the time. I would spend all my free time with these so-called friends. I always had the will to do good, but for some reason I didn't want to. This was where the mask takes place. I thought I was invisible which enabled me and kept me in hindrance. I found out the hard way who my real friends were. *All my homies seem to change their faces.*

I wore the mask, but I was barely conscious of it. I knew that under difficult circumstances I changed my demeanor, but I thought of it as normal. If I felt threatened or funny, I would put this mask on. With it on, I didn't care about anything. I played the hard role and intimidated people. I figured if they were scared of me then they would give me respect. But the truth is you can't force or make people respect you. But for some reason, I continued this behavior.

I also experienced sex at a young age. I liked the feeling so I carried onward in it. I had a lot of girlfriends and was called a player. (This means that I played girls for fools, talking to more than one at a time.) This was all in my adolescence and early teens. I also was introduced to alcohol and drugs. Just like sex, I enjoyed it, so I continued to participate. The reason I like to do this was because it all gave me a feeling of invisibility. I would drink and smoke some weed and be in my own world. I loved this feeling. I kept all of this from my parents in fear of repercussions. This, in my opinion, is what separated my parents and me, but I was oblivious to it and didn't take notice. I changed because of my drug use and other experiences.

I ran the streets as if I owned them with my so called "homies." It seemed like I went from small things to bigger things quickly. When I say this, I mean I went from little kid fights to sex and from sex to drugs and from drugs to, finally, crimes. I was in a bad circle of friends. It's like I wanted to get out of it, but I didn't want out bad enough!

I take full responsibility for my actions, but I was misled also. I had a strong head, but let myself get sucked into the wrong behavior. My environment or surroundings kept me mentally imprisoned. When I tell others this, they say "if you're so smart why did you let others suck you in?" My answer to those whose mind wonders is that I was young-minded and had a "sense to belong" just like everyone else. I could have beaten the odds and veered away, but would I be who I am today? Of course not! Like my mother used to tell me, the Lord works in mysterious ways.

I remember when I was 13 years old my mother shared with me that my father wasn't my biological dad. At this time, there was so many questions running through my consciousness. I was so occupied that I didn't notice the change in my demeanor.

I was already getting into difficult situations, but now my behavior intensified. I would get into petty arguments with my parents and yell out that my father wasn't my real father. I would run away to friends' homes and stay there for awhile.

My parents provided for me, but I wanted the nicest of the nicest. I would strong-arm rob people so I could buy clothes on my own. I fought daily to keep my reputation of being tough. I felt like I had to do these things to fit in.

Now that I look back on my life, I can only tell you I did what I did because I felt it was legitimate. If a person ponders that something is wrong or right, it's because of the values and morals put in their heads at a young age. I felt there was nothing immoral about what I was doing. I felt like if I didn't get people first then they would get me. You feel me? I don't regret anything that I've done, because it's all contributed to my understanding that I hold now.

Having the demeanor I had, I visited my second home, Remann Hall, frequently. My first visit wasn't a good one because I rested in a cell waiting for my parents to come get me. I played the role and said that I was sorry. I was sorry because I got caught. But I continued my expedition in this strange and treacherous path, blind to the fact that the state was not going to put up with me for much longer. I carried on with my wrongdoing till I met up with a challenger that just wouldn't fold, "Juvenile Rehabilitation Administration" (JRA). I almost received institution time, but I waited until my trial and pleaded guilty for 2 months in juvenile. I was glad I didn't get the years they were trying to give me, but not humble like I should have been. After that I tried to maintain good behavior.

I still fought and did drugs, but I was like - *I'm cool on committing crimes.* I had had enough engagements with Remann Hall. I went down the straight line for a while but still turned down fallacious trails.

I was caught and arrested for 2 counts of Robbery, Initimidation of a Witness, and Felony Harassment. I didn't do everything for which I'm charged for, but I do take full responsibility for it. For those that wonder why? It's because I've done a lot in the past that fortunately I was never arrested for, and I am privileged to be alive and only serving juvenile life. I know what goes around comes around and I still have more coming to me.

Now that we have established some kind of . . . what should I call it? Relationship, I can tell you about the aftermath of that little kid who is now a young man. There is much more I've failed to tell you, but I would rather not. I can dwell on my past or move on. I chose to move on.

Where should I start? I guess I'll start from the day I was told that I would be incarcerated until my 21st birthday. May 13, 1999, my co-defendant was sentenced in front of me to juvenile life in a maximum security institution. I felt his pain but held in my feeling. Then I was told by a judge that I wouldn't walk another street for the next 5+ years, deprived of my adolescent life. When I questioned such actions, which I felt were excessive, I was told that I was a high risk, danger to community, and a menace to society. A menace to society. When the judge declared this, I believe my heart fell to the lowest depths possible.

Then there was silence. I heard a faint cry penetrate through the soundless environment. The cry increased its volume instantly. Then there was more that followed. My mother and my co-defendant's mom shared tears of sorrow.

At this time my mind searched for answers. The journey was unsuccessful. The boy who thought that he could take on the whole world fell short. I tasted a dose of my own medicine. I shed tears of pain and confusion.

I remember talking to my mother after the sentencing. Everything that she told me would happen if I continued to do wrong happened. I felt so weak and helpless. Instead of attempting to sort out the problem and change I chose the opposite route. I figured from what I was told about institutions I was going to have to prove myself.

Walking down the halls of my juvenile detention center, it seemed to take hours. I wasn't sure if my legs were virile enough to make the trip. I wiped my face, still wanting to look tough and keep striking. I remember my whole body felt heavy. I wanted someone to feel the pain I was going through. I finally made it to my destination. I waited for the door to open and walked slowly past everyone. I viewed the residents' mouths moving but heard no sound. I walked into my enclosed chamber and slammed the door shut. I fell on my bed and the mask I had been wearing for so long fell off. I no longer had enough energy to hold it on my face. The real me showed. I cried for God but received no answers. Rage built up inside of me. I lay on my bed frustrated, trying to sort out my life. Every time I made the attempt I was unsuccessful. I kept hearing my mother's sweet voice telling me to stop doing what I was doing. I wonder why I didn't listen.

Let me elaborate in depth about this mask. When I wear it, I'm fearless and I don't care about anything or anyone. I show no remorse and display such anger verbally and physically. When I don't have it on, I'm caring and real. I try to help out and I respect others.

The next day I was told that I was going to a maximum security institution (Maple Lane or Greenhill). I asked when and was informed that I'd be shipped away in a few days. I left Remann Hall on May 17th 1999 in shackles as if I were an untame animal. The drive was a little longer than an hour. I tried to store as many memories of the outside as possible knowing I wouldn't be out for a while. Encaged at the age of 15 for the rest of my juvenile life.

I was placed in the intensive management unit (IMU) building on the orientation side. There they told me I would stay there from 15 days to 45 days then be placed into population (open campus). I learned about the programs Maple Lane provided. I behaved for the first week and then went back behind the mask that got me in my situation. I was frustrated and wanted to take the easy way out.

After the first week, I was tired of this place and being so good, so I started acting up. Why be good when I'm locked up doing 5 years? I picked a fight with the biggest individual in the unit. I won the fight and was praised by my peers. For some reason I needed such acclaim behind this mask.

I proceeded on with my villain type conduct. I hit open campus and saw a couple of familiar faces. I stayed quiet at first, not really knowing how to act. I made associates quickly but kept my distance. I did fairly well at first but, just like on the outs, I started acting up.

I began to change thanks to my mother's strong will to help me. I found myself in lock-up a few times though, all for fighting. In lock-up I only came out of my cell for 1 hour a day. In there, I had plenty of time to evaluate myself. I learned the most being incarcerated. I learned that life aint fair and my homies only lead me to the dark.

A homie is a phony in this world of stress.

Just like my dad told me, them dudes called my friends would only be around as long as the fun was around. My so-called friends only wrote me a couple of times this whole time I've been in here. The only ones that write are family and ex-girlfriends. Honestly, those guys I hung around didn't let me down, they just showed their true colors. My best friends are two special people named Eugena and Cedric Stanley, my parents!

On September 24, 1999, I was released from lock-up to never return again. I had spent enough time in the IMU during that month. I had found out who I was, Johnathan Dowand Smith! Not that guy running around causing mayhem. I was in lock-up for 35 days. I returned to open campus and slipped up a little bit, but I am maintaining. Slowly but surely I am really changing for the good. I stopped caring what others thought.

A young man in here taught me some things, and he didn't even know he was doing it. I learned from his progress and also my parents' support. I started to set goals and plans for my future, and by doing so, I prospered. My mother continued to help me and carry me when I was weak. The mask that I had grown so close to started to fall off, and when it did, I annihilated it for good!

I feel like I have come so far, and finally, I am living an orthodox life, you feel me? I might get into a quarrel here and there, but who doesn't? I'm not saying I changed quickly, but I did change. It's hard, too, because every day is a new test, but I do my best!

I've spent two birthdays behind bars, and I'm not proud of that. What I'm proud of is my progress and the commitment to help myself and others. Please recognize that I've only chosen to share a fraction of my life. There is much more that I didn't share, but my fingers wouldn't be able to handle such an assignment.

It is now June of 2000, and I've been doing great. I plan to maintain for the next 3 1/2 years. Who knows, one of you readers out there might run into me later in life.

I must say that Maple Lane and my situation changed my ways. I am a changed person.

In my enclosed chamber or cell, I've attained so much knowledge and not only have I benefited from it but so have my peers! I could have dwelled on all unfair unjust acts - *just us blacks*. I have faced being incarcerated, but I decided not to. I wanted you readers out there to hear my part in all this confusion, you feel me? Life goes on! Right?

I hope you've enjoyed walking with my shadows. *Follow my footsteps where it's shallow and you hear our sorrows and aint no promises of tomorrows.* I also hope my story has touched someone out there that might be headed down the same path. I don't glorify nothing I've done I'm just speaking the real. For my struggling soldiers out there I feel your pain, but it's time for a change! You feel me? If you're not hearing your parents, then please hear me! I've been through it all and probably more so, I'm just trying to help. I found out the hard way that my only friends, real friends, that is, are my Mother and Father. Just keep in mind that a friend wouldn't lead a friend to danger, and it is better to have one friend than a crowd full of smiling strangers! You feel me? . . . Well, do you? I've been asking you this whole time.

Aftermath

I'm working on my problems and weaknesses while I'm incarcerated. I can see my goals being addressed and achieved. I have 3 years and 3 months left, and that's a long time. But I plan to have a lot going for me when I get out. My release date is December 18, 2003. When I go to school, I'm going to study Business Management, Media Communication, and Music. I plan to make it in the music industry. I will because I'm going to work for it. It's going to be hard, but I can do it. My mind's no longer on friends, clothes, and being popular. I'm too busy working on my self and my goals to become successful.

I've prayed to my Lord for a chance, and I know it will come. It's as simple as that. I'm no longer looking through a tunnel. My eyes are wide open. I never knew that my goals could take up all my time. I still live by faith and not time so I'll just take it step by step.

Overall, I'm doing good, and I just wanted you guys to hear the most recent update on how I'm doing. Thanks again for listening. I'll leave you guys with this - Remember me when you see me on MTV and BET as Johnathan D Smith aka BLAZON. I'll leave you guys with this last thought:

It's hard manuvering through this complex maze without any directions. You have to move quick at times and choose the right paths. If you make a mistake, shake it off and keep striking. Look at every situation as a learning experience and grow from it. Once you find out who you are, then you'll realize your purpose.

Do you know who you are?

Wake Up

Wake up. Is there fear inside of you?
You long to belong and do what you see others do.
Look deep inside of you.
Only you know if your heart is true.
Strive hard and obstacles will break through,
Hard times disappear right in front of you.
Wake up. There is fear inside of you.

THE RISE FROM THE MUCKLESHOOT REZ

FLOYD GONZALEZ

My life story aint gonna tell you what to do. You make your own choices. My life story is just gonna tell you that going down a dark road is gonna do nothing but cause you trouble. I'm writing this cause I want to see more people from the ghetto go down the road with light and happiness and not always having to watch their back.

I grew up on the Muckleshoot rez in Auburn, Washington just about all my life. There I felt good because I was around people I was close to. Most of the people on the rez was like my family, because we took care of each other. That made me feel good cause I knew there was someone there for me. I'm proud to be NATIVE American because my people are so few. And they're strong and spiritual people. And a lot of them in the old days got killed off by the Europeans. My people are survivors. That's another reason why I'm so proud to be NATIVE. After all my people been through, we continue to thrive.

My life story aint gonna tell you what to do. You make your own choices. My life story is just gonna tell you that going down a dark road is gonna do nothing but cause you trouble. I'm writing this cause I want to see more people from the ghetto go down the road with light and happiness and not always having to watch your back. But you do what you want.

I remember when I was a little kid I put my hand on a hot stove cause I wanted some more food. It burnt the hell out of my hand and my hand hurt for about a week. I learned never put your hand on the stove. Ask for what you want, and you won't go through all the hurt and suffering.

I have happy memories of growing up on the rez or what I think was happy memories. I think it was fun in ways but there was other times I would sit there and wonder why all the drama was happening.

Like the drinking and drugs. That's a big problem on a lot of rezes. I think it was bad on the Muckleshoot rez cause that's where I was. I remember my mom and my Auntie Penny and my Uncle Bud, they always got drunk together. My uncle Bud would get mad and start to yell and start putting holes through the walls. Me and my cuzin Budsy would sit there and laugh at him, and he would get mad at us and try to scare us but we knew he wouldn't do shit to us. But there was more than just that. A lot of people would get killed cause they would be walking down the road and someone wouldn't see them cause he or she would be drunk and they would hit them. I think the hardest times in the rez was seeing my mom and other family get drunk and fight with each other.

I don't remember much when my mom and dad were together, but I remember when me and my cuzin Budsy burned down this house. It was fun while it lasted. But when my Auntie and my mom found out it was worse than bein' in this jail cell. My mom and auntie beat my cuzin's ass as I watched from the woods, thinking they would be tired. I walked out and got my ass beat with a big ass piece of wood. It seemed to me that my mom would never stop, but when she did it seemed like she beat my ass around the clock. It was night time when the fire went out. We all jut sat there and watched, and me and my cuzin got laughed at and talked about.

On the rez, it's a pretty crazy place to grow up because it ain't the same rules that the white community goes by. On Muckleshoot rez, there was no tribal cops till like '96. So there was no getting arrested for being drunk, for getting in a fight, for driving down the street fast. That's why a lot of white people, not just whites but blacks, Natives and any other people, drove up the hill from Auburn to get away from the cops because we were out of their arresting area.

So a lot of bad stuff happened up on the rez. A lot of people didn't practice our culture. There was lots of alcohol and drug abuse going on. I started smoking weed when I was 7 or 8 years old, started to drink when I was 11 years-old. Me and my cuzin Budsy was stealing weed from our moms. We would smoke weed with his brother. We got caught a couple of times, we would get a beating but would still smoke. Me and my cuzin were little bad asses, hard headed, didn't listen and we still don't in ways. Because on the rez, there wasn't the rules that we have to follow now.

So when we left the rez, we left with the same rez boys. We were the little bad asses that didn't give a damn. We went to tribal school. We did bad there. We would get it cause our Aunties were the school teachers, and after school, we would get it from our moms. I remember the fun we had, but it was nothing but trouble. Like I remember when we was all standing at the lower end of the tribal housing by where I lived with my uncle. We were all throwing rocks at this big ass bees' nest. Everybody, all the kids, we was throwing rocks. Me and my older cuzin Danny moved up a little closer. We're throwing rocks, but they're hitting the outside of the house. The nest was right in the corner of the house. The last rock I throw hits the nest, the nest falls on the ground, everyone goes running. Me and my cuzin get right in front of our house, and I get stung. I fell on the ground, rolling around, thinking I'm dying. It's funny now that I think about it, but when I was little I was wishin' I hadn't thrown that rock.

There was this other time me and my cuzin Budsy and my sister and some other cuzins were standing on the hill that leads down to the highway. This is another one where I'm throwing rocks. We're up on the hill throwing rocks at the cars that go by. We don't care if we broke a window or anything like that. The worst that could have happened is us breaking one of our Auntie's or Uncle's windows. I throw this big rock that I had to pick up with both hands. I throw it over the little ledge that we were standing on, and the rock went right through a cop's window. We were all scared cause we heard what they did to people off the rez. The cop comes up there askin' who threw the rock. On his way down he's getting more rocks thrown at his car. He comes down and asked us if we were the ones that threw the rocks. We all lied and said no. My mom seen the cop talking to us and comes out yelling, tells the cop he better get out before something bad happened. Because where I grew up, white people that went on the rez was known not to come off the rez. At least not walkin'. They left in a body bag. He told my mom what happened. She said she would deal with it. So he leaves. My mom comes straight to me. I'm scared she's gonna whoop my ass, but she didn't. That didn't mean she still wasn't mad. Because when I got caught throwing rocks at cars again she beat my butt pretty bad. Whenever I did something she told me not to do, I would get a worse beating than the first one.

My mom, she was a nice lady that cared about all of her kids, that's why she beat my ass so hard when I got in trouble. I used to think she did it cause she was havin' fun doing it. But now I sit in this cell dwelling on all the stuff she ever told me. There was times when I would get it when I didn't do anything, but my cuzin Budsy didn't want to be the only one to get beat. There was times I did the same to him.

Some time in my life we moved off the rez. I dwell on that, too. A lot of bad stuff happened then. We lived with my sister's dad for a little bit. I was still the same little bad ass, but now I was in the city. We lived in south Seattle. I don't remember any of the schools' names, but at school I did bad. I was bad, then I was badder, then I was stupid. Then I was just locked up.

The South End was almost like the rez, but there was Blacks, Asians, Whites, Mexicans, and some Natives. I didn't like white people all my life. I was little and we would hear people (Natives) talking about white people and how they were bad people, don't trust them. So I did what I heard. I got along with the Asians real good, there would be some blacks I got along with like the ones that lived on the same block I lived on. They were just like me, didn't like whites. We would beat them up. It got to the point where I didn't like white people at all. I just had a hate for all white people. There was times I wanted to kill some people for shit they did to me but as I got older I found out all white people aint like that. So I got closer and closer to some white folks. Don't get me wrong, there are still some white people I don't like. There's just a bunch of racists out there that don't have respect for themselves or other races. So they get to be racists to other races like Asians, blacks, NATIVES whatever. All that shit I went through when I was younger only made me stronger. So I wasn't losing at all, I was only gaining more strength.

One day my mom's friends came over and we all left. I don't remember where we went, but she was asking where my sister was. Me not knowin' any better said she was with her nigger boyfriend. I said that cause the people I lived around was black and I heard them saying Nigga when they talked, calling each other Nigga. But my mom's friend looked at my mom and said -What did he say? And I said it again. My mom told her to whoop my ass. We're driving down the street, and my mom's friend is hitting me, she hit me like 3 times and

I got down behind her seat, then my mom started to hit me. That's one word I never said, I still don't say it and I don't like to hear other people saying it. Even black people.

There's another time she and my mom beat my ass. We just got back from the rez. We were at Muckleshoot for a week. We get back to Seattle, I was getting out of the car, I seen my mom get out and everyone else get out on the other side. Just me and my mom's friend get out of the driver's side. But her daughter was getting out right after me. I didn't know. I go to shut the door and slam her hand in the door. I broke her hand and wrist. I go to tell my mom, and they take her to the hospital. They came back, and I got another ass beating. I tried to tell them it was not on purpose, but they didn't believe me. When I say ass beating I don't mean abuse, I mean a whoopin'.

I remember the day my gramma died like it was yesterday. Me and my sister and my little brother went to go visit her, it was a hot day. I think me and my sister went and picked blackberries so she could make jam. We come back to visit for a little bit, and mom said we had to leave. Me, I was the one that was ready, because I didn't think Grams liked me too much. She would give chocolate to my sister and little brother while I was outside, or she would hide it from me when she gave it to them. Well, I was ready to leave. My sisters were trying to stay longer. We left, and like a couple hours later, I guess she died. She didn't take her medication. It was up on the fridgerator, and she was too short to get it even if she tried.

My mom, she drank a lot so I didn't learn that much about my Native people. I know that white people was like a enemy to us, though. I remember I would learn in the white schools about how the whites won the wars they had with the Natives. One day while we were living in some section eight housing, she got me and my brother cowboys and Indian toys. I would make it so the Indians would always win. I had dreams, visions that I was in the old days learning how to be a warrior. When I would wake up, I sometimes cried cause my mom would tell me my dreams won't happen in these days. She told me the whites took that from me. That made me not like white people even more.

I don't know how this happened or when, I think it was in 1990 we moved to Sumner, it's over by Auburn, Tacoma. We moved there with my mom's friend Becky. I still ain't changed none. I start going to school getting in even more trouble, cause out of the whole school there was 5 people that wasn't white. 2 Natives, 1 Black and an Asian and a Mexican. The kids were racist, and I was bein' racist right back. They would call me injun, I would call them white bread or honcky. I was in trouble with the teacher a lot too. I would throw my desk at them to let my anger out. Us five minorities stuck together. I got in a lot of fights, then I started to get kicked out of school. There was some white kids that I liked, but they really wasn't nothing. We would just use them for their toys. Then one day, out of nowhere, we moved to Tacoma.

I'm doin a little better but after I got to know some kids, back to trouble I was. We stayed there, I would say, a year, then we moved back to Sumner. We stayed there. It was summer. I think we stayed till school started back up, then we moved to Benney Lake right up the hill from Sumner. The people we was living with, their kids were just like me, always in trouble. I got along with them white people, then they moved to Arizona, and my mom was paying rent. She started going out with this white dude. He was cool. He let me smoke and stay up as long as I wanted. Then one day, he started to be mean. I think my mom got mad cause he let us do whatever we wanted.

I started to do better with white people because that's what was all around me except one Asian family. But I was still doin' bad. I had all the white kids doin' bad with me. We would all go to the store and steal, I got them throwing rocks at cars, stealing bikes, breaking windows in houses. My closest white friends are still my friends today, but we had our times when we fought. I beat this one white kid up really bad and after that they were all scared of me. They thought, and still think, I'm crazy.

I remember there was this old man, I would clean his yard in the summer and winter so I would have money. It wasn't a lot, it was 5 bucks. He kept his pop and junk food outside, like his candy and stuff. This old man made the wrong choice by letting me know this. Every night my lil' crew would go over there and steal his stuff, but we wouldn't steal a lot so he wouldn't know.

I did a lot of bad stuff in Benney Lake. Me and my sister beat this one girl up and burned her on the face like 6 times with a cigarette. I would kill people's cats, because on the rez there was no cats cause every time someone had one we would kill it and feed it to our dogs. So I didn't like cats, because that's what I was taught, just like I was taught to be racist. There was a lot of people in Benney Lake that didn't like our family cause of me, it was like that everywhere I lived.

We moved from B.L. and moved to Aberdeen with my mom's boyfriend because his son died, and that's where he's from. I was glad because he would make us do all kinds of work. We didn't live in Aberdeen that long, maybe a year. I was like 8 or 9. We stayed with his ex-wife. We were living on the south side for a little bit. Then my mom wanted to get her own place, so we moved on to the East side. Pretty ghetto, but all Aberdeen is a ghetto. I started hanging out with this Native cat. We got to doing the same stuff I been doing all my life. We stealing from the mall, we smoking weed. Then we start going to this pool hall across the street from his mom's house. I learn how to play, I'm good. Then one day, my mom and her boyfriend want to move to Auburn. So we move to Auburn.

We move there to the same place my gramma used to live. Now, the place is really ghetto. There's crack heads all over the place. There's gangbangers all over the place. I started hangin' out with the crowd that's like me. Well, my sister was kickin it with them. She knew them cause they used to sell weed to my cuzins. I knew them a little bit, not much. But I start to kick it with these cats on a regular basis. These guys are getting me high and drunk. My home boy Paul gets me into selling drugs. I'm 10 years old selling dope to 40 year olds, you know I'm loving this life. I'm getting everything I want.

We go back to Aberdeen and we're there for a little bit, I'm still kickin it with the Native cat. We're going to these Mexican dances. I start messing with all these girls, lying by telling them I'm 15 years old. I'm doing a lot more partyin'. My mom's at home stressin' cause I ain't goin' home, I'm stayin' with the homiez.

Then one day this guy named Steve called the cops on me and my lil' brother while we was in the pool hall playin' pool. Cops come. Search us cause I was drinkin' and I was high all the night before and that morning. They don't find nothing of mine. They couldn't find no alcohol because I had a mixed drink and the homie took it when he left. They take me and my brother to the C.P.S. It was in '94, the state took us away from my mom.

Summer of 95

I remember this one time I was selling dope in a dopehouse. It was the summer of 95. I think I was twelve. Well, me and my homeboy Casper, who was 16, we was making a lot of money. There were a lot of dope fiends. I remember a lady came in with three kids. One two-year old, a four-year old, and an eight-year old. I don't remember what the lady's name was or what she looks like. I just remember what the eight-year old kid told me after I sold his mama some heroin. He told me he didn't like me cause I sold his mama drugs. After he told me this, he hit me. At the time, I was a really greedy person. I didn't really care what the kid liked.

But now that I think of it, I know how he was feeling cause my mama did drugs. It got me somewhere in my heart. That's the only reason I remember it, and that's the only reason I'm writing about it. I didn't care really about the lady or her three kids because I had to make money so I could eat.

Chillie Pimp

This is a Chillie Pimp story I'm just telling it cause I want people to know all the different things I been through.

Me, my cuzin Nish, and my mom's boyfriend John was in the house talking, just bullshitting. Bout anything and everything. Main thing we was talking bout was what we was gonna do that night. My cuzin says his girl was comin over and she was gonna bring some friends. My mom's boyfriend was getting some coca and crank. He had some friends comin over too. Well, at the same time I was thinking bout weed. So, I told them I was gonna call my cuzin Robbie, Nish's younger brother. So I go across the street and call him from the payphone at the Exxon station. I rap with him for a little bit, asking if he was gonna bring some weed cause he sell weed. He said he was gonna. Then we hung the phone up.

I look down the street and see this tall white girl bout 5'11", long blonde hair. She was walking towards me. I walk back to the house and tell my cuzin Nish. I thought it was his bitch cuz his girl was tall with blonde hair. He goes to the door and sees her and said that wasn't her. She's at the same payphone I was just at.

I tell Nish and John that I'm bout to fuck that bitch. It wasn't Nish's girl. So I go over to the payphone where she's at. She hangs the phone up and I started to talk to her. She asked me who I was. And I tell her my tag name: "Li'l Man." She tells me her name was Amanda. Somewhere in there my age got brought up and I told her I was 15 bout to be 16. I was just lyin to her. I was really 12. She said she was 20. She said she had to leave but told me to come over. She gave me her address. I said I'd be there.

I went back across the street to my mama's house and told Nish and John she wanted me over to her house. Nish told me to quit telling some jive ass story, that girl don't want shit to do with you. I said OK. We'll see when she comes home with me tonight.

At 10:00pm I got to Amanda house. We were talking about a lot of stuff. I was trying to fuck, but she was saying, -Just friends for now. I was like OK. Just friends then. I asked her if she wanted to come to our New Year's party. At first she said no, and then I got her to come. She wasn't doing shit anyways. So we got to my house at 11:45. We got pretty messed up, I don't even remember how much we drank or smoked or snorted. I know we did a lot.

My cuzin Ben was trying to mack on Amanda, but she told him she didn't want to be with him. Ben got all mad and leaves. Just about everybody's passed out. I don't know what happened after that cause I tried to down a fifth of gin and I passed out. It was about 4:30am.

It's been 3 weeks since I seen Amanda so I go over to her house. She lived 3 blocks away so I walked. I get there, knock on the door. She opens the door and has a big smile on her face. She tells me to come in. I sit on the couch and we talk. We just talked about what we been doing and why I ain't seen her. She didn't want to come over cause my cuzin was being rude. She didn't know if he would be over so she didn't come over. She asked me if I wanted a drink. I said yes. She goes in the kitchen, comes out 5 min later. I didn't know she meant hard alcohol and I downed it and almost got sick cause I didn't know it was a mixed drink. We drink more and get pretty drunk. She only had a fifth and it wasn't even full. We drank it all, there was no more to drink so I break out some weed. She told me she didn't smoke weed, which was not hard to believe. Cause she almost choked to death.

Well, we were sitting there and she tells me bout going into the room to get something. I wait. Ain't no one home. Her mom was gone somewhere. Her dad don't live with them, and she was a only child.

After a little bit she tells me to come in the room so I stagger my way to the room. We talk a little bit. She started to kiss me. I was rubbing my hand in between her legs. She started to take my shirt and pants off. I started to do the same to her.

We fucked for about two hours, and she walked me to my house. After that day we started to see each other. We did a lot of fun stuff. She started smoking weed more often. And then one day I got her hooked on H. She got into it really bad. Before, and while we were together, I was selling H and C. So, I could give her a fix when she needed one. But then one day when I was selling dope to this one white dude named Tommy, I got robbed for all my money and dope. So I couldn't give her dope anymore. She started doing crimes to get it. She got scared she was gonna get caught. Amanda came to me asking me what she should do. Me, I really didn't know anything for her to do that wouldn't get her in jail. Amanda told me she was getting dope sick. I told her I know of one thing she could do. I said I don't think you would want to do it. She said she would do anything for a fix.

I told her it was easy money. Then she really wanted to do it.

THIS IS THE START OF THE CHILLIE PIMP.

We left the house, started our way to downtown Aberdeen to a bar called Mack's. There was a lot of whores and drug users and dealers there. We got to Mack's. She asked what we was doing down there. I said you wanted to get your dope? Amanda said yes. I told her she was gonna be a whore. At first she didn't want to do it. She started to cash bad checks for a couple weeks, got caught for that, went to jail for a night. The courts said she had to come back for court. The night she got out she came and told me what happened and said she wanted to go down on the track. We went down to Mack's, and she started to whore. She was talking with some other whores, and they hooked her up with some tricks (guys that pay for a fuck or blow jobs). Her first trick came to her and she started talking to him. I guess he said something sick cause she said to get away from her. Then she comes and tells me. I tell her she can't just be passing up tricks that want to spend money. She says OK. 10 minutes pass by, a little Mexican comes over to her and asks, "how much?" and she tells him. They go over to his car, they do their thang. She comes back and gives me the money. Goes back on the track. Amanda pulled a lot of tricks cause she's new and young and that's what the tricks like and want. She keeps doing this, and she gets the tricks to think I'm her little brother. She told them she was doing this to take care of me cause our mom and dad left us. The tricks were giving her more money than she asked for. The tricks were buying me shoes and clothes, then giving her more money to spend on me, plus the money she was getting for the sexual stuff.

She was making a lot of money. There was this one guy named Bob. He would come pick her up just to be with her. He didn't always want sexual favors. She would stay with him all day. He would pay her $1,500 for the whole day. He was some kind of logger. He was pretty rich cause he'd come around in all his nice things, nice car. He told her he didn't like such a pretty girl out on the track. That's why he gave her so much money. She told me this but I didn't care. Cause with me its money first, then a girl. So I didn't care how she got it just that she got it.

Well, she's living with me at my mama's house. My mama knows what she's doing and she don't like it cause my mama did that when she was younger. She didn't get forced to do it, she just had to do it cause her husband didn't want to be with her no more cause she went to prison for drugs. That's why she did it. She doesn't like it at all. So she tells me to tell Amanda that if she wants to live with us she has to help pay rent and help clean up around the house. I go and tell Amanda. She said to tell my mama to piss off and she wasn't gonna do shit around the house. I had to put hands on her cause she was being disrespectful to my mama. After that I went into the room with my mama and we smoke some weed. My mama tells me Amanda has to move out then. I said if my bitch has to move we gonna go to a motel room and live. Mama got all mad because I didn't stay home. I left with the bitch.

The whole next week went good. Amanda did her thang, I did mine. One night, I don't remember what day it was. But I remember it was a little after 5:00pm. I asked her if she been using condoms. She tells me she always uses condoms. She said that I was the only one she didn't use them with. Just because, I gave her NINE of them. I put them in these bags she be carrying around and told her she better use them. She said -I will, don't worry, baby.

So we go down to Mack's and she does what she's best at. She pulls her NINE tricks and we were on our way. I grab her bag out her hands and look in it and said -What the hells wrong with you? She tried to lie to me and said they had condoms that's why she didn't use the ones I gave her. I was all mad at her cause the bitch was lying. I started walking and I go to the pool hall right around the corner from Mack's where I hung around a lot. I talked to this girl Bridget that works at the pool hall. Amanda comes in all rude and starts talking to me. I smack her and Bridget tells us one of you guys have to leave. I told Amanda she better leave or when I seen her I was gonna beat her ass. Amanda leaves.

Me and Bridget start talking again. She asked me why I was doing this stuff I was doing. I told her I was in love with money. Bridget tells me I should get married to a girl that gots lots of money and I should get a job and I would have lots of money and wouldn't have to be watching my back all the time. I tell Bridget -GangStaz don't get married, they hustle till they die. It's all about money not marriage. She got mad at me and asked if I would leave or go upstairs and play pool. Me and Bridget were hella cool.

My boy Black, he was a pimp. I say "was" because he got killed. Fucking with the wrong bitch, I guess. But I looked up to him cause I wanted everything he had. Three cars. Nice little place. Lots of gold. And didn't have to worry bout anything but the police. That's what I wanted. I was sitting there thinking all this time this bitch did something wrong or if she wouldn't do something that I wanted her to do, I would beat the bitch. I really thought I was a pimp.

We stayed together some time. She's still whoring. She's getting really bad into the H dope. I'm starting to feel a little sorry. I try to tell her to quit doing dope. She said she tried and couldn't. I start to think about what she told me when we first started seeing each other. Amanda told me she was pregnant. I was thinking, if this girl had my baby, it would come out with a missing arm or something. She had a miscarriage. I was glad of that cuz I didn't want to have a messed up baby, and plus, I was too young to be having any kids. I wanted her to quit doing dope because she was really looking bad but she wouldn't. We moved to Seattle. She was still whoreing, making good money because she was fucking with them dyke bitches too. She got pregnant again. I made her get rid of it. She wanted to keep it because she thought it would get her to stop doing dope.

I was getting really greedy with the money. So I said - I don't care anymore about your dope habit. We went back to Aberdeen for a little bit. I said we was gonna move back. She said, why we moving? We only stayed in Seattle for three months. I want to move back and you're coming with me. So we go back to Seattle and get our shit and left. We got back in the Motel where we stayed. When we moved back I got deep into coca and crack, more crack, though I was shooting up a lot. I started not giving a fuck. I didn't give a fuck about nobody. This went on for a couple more months.

4th of July

Later, I stayed with my cuzin Stephie in Auburn, I did my thang, she did hers. I partied the whole time. She said if I didn't come home by 12am don't come, cause I wasn't getting in. On July 7th, I was at her house, she said if I needed any money just come ask. She would give me some. I go and ask her. She tells me to go ask her husband. I do and he gives me $20. But I wanted more. I pushed him and took his wallet and left. I went to my homeboyz Joe and Dave's house. We wanted to get some weed and crank. My plan for the next day was to go back to Aberdeen because I knew I had money there, and I would be able to pay my cuzin back.

Next day, we went over to Joe and Dave's house. We got some crank and weed. Josh had some gin, Mad Dog 20/20, Brady, some other stuff. And I still don't go back to Aberdeen. It's the eleventh now, and I'm at the river getting all messed up. Well, the homegirl Casey said she wanted to leave and aint nobody want to take her back home, so I do. We walking and I said -Let's go over to the homegirl Honey's house. She said alright. So we walk over there and I guess my cuzin's boyfriend seen me go into Honey's house. My cuzin knows Honey, they're good friends. So he goes and calls Stephie and tells her I'm at Honey's house. Well, we're just kicking it, me, Casey, Honey, KGB, Rich John, some other people I didn't really know. We're all bullshitting and the next thing I know is I heard a loud ass bang on the door. We all thought it was the police, everyone's hiding their dope and hiding. I was out in the backyard and my homeboy Rich was like - It's all good, it aint the police.

So, I walk in and the next thing I know, my cuzin Stephie is yelling at me. Before I took her husband's wallet, I broke into her brother's fireworks stand and took just about everything in there. She was saying - Who the hell you think you are just going around stealing from your family?

I was dumbfounded because she made me look like a fool in front of all my homiez. She told me to go get in the car. We're going back to her house. I was like fuck that. I aint doing shit. My homegirl Honey told me to go. Don't bring troubles to her house. I go and I seen all my homiez that was at the river on their way back to Josh's house. They came to the car, and I told them I would be back later. We leave and Stephie is asking where the wallet was. I don't think she's that stupid to think I still had all the money or the wallet. So I tell her I threw it away. She got all mad and we stop at the Denny's and talk a little bit more. Then she calls the cops. I tried to take off, but Stephie's husband grabs my arm. I couldn't get out the door.

The cops come and handcuff me and put me in the back of their car. I could hear the cop talking to Stephie. They ask if they want to press charges. My cuzin said no. She started to talk to her boyfriend in Spanish and then she said she wanted to cuz she wanted me to learn a lesson. The lady cop comes and tells me I was going to juvy. She would have let me go, but I already had a warrant out. So she had to take me in. She goes and talks to Stephie again. While she is talking to her, I put the money and dope I had on me in my shoe under the sole. I had $500 in cash and like a $1000 in dope. The lady comes back and we leave. She asked me why I did it. I didn't give her a reason, just said cause I was drunk.

I get to the DYS (Department of Youth Services) and they put me in intake for the night cause I was drunk and high. I'm sitting in there thinking. I'm one fool for not going back to Aberdeen when I said I was gonna.

They take me to the hall where everyone goes when they first get to DYS. I was there for a little bit, waiting my trial. I was doing good making my levels till this one cat, JR, started to mess with me. We were sitting in the day area watching BET, a music show. And this fool gonna put his foot next to my face. I ask him to move his feet. He didn't, so I push them away. He puts them back up by my head. I didn't do nothing - I was like shit. If he touch me with his feet, I'm gonna get in a fight with him. The next thing I know I'm feeling this cat's feet touch my face. I get up and tell his little bitch ass to get up and go to the bathroom. He didn't. He just sits there and talks shit. When I was younger I used to be down with the Nortenoz 14, a Mexican gang. He started to dis my homiez, my dead homiez at that. So I just took off on his little bitch ass. I was getting off on his ass, the staff came and I stop cause I didn't want to get slammed. But they slammed me anyways then put me in my room. We were talking shit out our doors planning for our next fight. Then staff comes and talks to me asking why we got in a fight. I told him cause he was kicking me in the head, and then he started to dis on my dead homiez. They go talk to him and come back. They said he said it was a whole different reason. He said we were rivals and I started to dis his hood calling him a crab and shit like that. But they said I was gonna get 72 hours and moved out of the Hall.

Well, they come to get me to go to Echo Glen. The whole time I was in DYS I had the $500 and my dope. But I got a visit and gave the dope to the homie Tony. His mom said she was my mom and he was my brother so they could come visit. I was gonna give him the money but I was like, no, I'm gonna keep it. The lady that came and told me I was going to Echo Glen said when I turn 14 I was going to Maple Lane. I was like cool, I had a lot of homiez up here at that time.

They come to bring me to Echo Glen and dude strip-searched me to make sure I didn't have anything I wasn't supposed to have. He found my money and told me they couldn't bring it cause I had too much. So they was gonna keep it there. I was like -Cool. Cause he said they was gonna send it in like a week.

So we leave. We go all over before going to Echo Glen. We go pick up a bunch of other people, drop a bunch of people off, then we dropped some dude off at Indian Ridge. I don't even know where we're at, then the next thing I know we're driving right past the homegirl Honey's house in Auburn. She lived right below the high-way and I guess you can go through Auburn to get to Echo Glen. After I seen her house and the homie KGB, Rich, and John sitting outside smoking, that made me want to go AWOL.

I was talking to the dude that was from Greenhill that was going to court in Tri-cities. He said it was easy to AWOL. So I was really pumped up about that. We get to the road that goes to Echo and I remember when my CPS worker was taking me to treatment in Spokane we stopped there for me to use the bathroom. He was telling me if I didn't straighten up I was gonna end up here. I was thinkin'-Fuck that muthafucka, he jinxed me.

We drive down the big long road that you go down to get to the main building. We get there, they ask me all kinds of stuff, then they tell me to sit on the couch. I was sitting there thinking bout running, it was going through my head like a racehorse. But I didn't do it. Then some guy comes and talks to me, I don't remember his name cause I didn't care who he was. I talked to him and he asks me about all the trouble I was getting into in DYS, I told him it was because there was people messing with me and starting fights with me. I told him I wasn't no bitch. He said -That's why you're going to Maple Lane when you turn 14. He told me he was going to put me in a maximum security cottage cause I was a trouble maker. I get to a quiet room and security comes and does a strip search and then puts handcuffs and leg chains on my legs.

One night my roommate Rigo came in all mad. I was on 24 hours and he came in talking shit about stuff. I tried to talk to him and he started to talk shit to me saying I was a drunken Indian and a bunch of shit like that. I would say he was a drunken Mexican. I wasn't getting mad about it. We was just arguing over stupid shit cause he was mad at staff.

Well, he gets to saying more shit and I told him to shut up. He got up and started talking shit about my family and friends, I told him to shut up, I didn't want to fight him cause we were cool. He wanted to fight though. He kicked me in the side. I was laying down on my bed when this happened. I told him I wasn't gonna fight him. I told him he wasn't mad at me, he was mad at staff. Then the next thing I know this mothafucka spits on me. I got up, we started to push each other around then we started to fight. I slammed him on my bed, and I kneed him in the face and punched him like six times. Then he slammed me in the door, and I pushed him in the wall. We were making hella noise. This was at dinner, everyone was eating. Some dude said that we were fighting and staff came in. They told me to sit on the bed. I did. They brought Rigo to a quiet room, then they brought me to one. The next day I go back and the staff talk to me and tell me I'm going back to maximum. I was like -cool, I wanted to go back anyhow. I go back, and Mrs. B talks to me. She asks why I went up there and acted a fool. I told her what happened, she told me she didn't believe me cause she worked with Rigo for a year. I told her -Whatever, I know what happened.

Well, like a week later, they told me I had to go to treatment or boot camp. I had three days to make up my mind. I told them I wasn't going to do nothing or go anywhere. On the third day, I told them I would go to boot camp. I go. And it's like I was in a new world. I got all these freaks in my face telling me what to do. Me, not liking to do what other people tell me to do, get slammed cause I wasn't trying to do any push-ups. Gangstaz don't do push-ups. They was gonna to put me in a little quiet room till the DC came and talked to me. He gets me to go back out there. I'm standing on line and this asshole DI comes at me all crazy telling me to do push-ups, then sit-ups, jumping jacks. Just a bunch of shit like that. I'm doing them, but not his speed. He tells me to stand on line and he gets to yelling at me. I was mugging him hella crazy. I told him he better get the fuck out of my face. I aint yo kid. That day was pretty crazy. I did a lot of push-ups.

I was hella mad. They made me cut my hair. But I got used to it, just like the push-ups and everything else they made me do. I got in a couple of fights there. I got in one with this Native cat. He was messing with me, and I took his stuff and threw it across the room. He went to hit me, and I ducked and hit him on the face and a couple of other places.

On October 11th, I was just sitting there talking with the homie and my counselor comes and tells me I'm gonna be on intensive parole. I was hella mad cause that messed up all my plans. Well, I get out of Echo Glen on the 13th. I really didn't want to go cause I knew it would feel hella weird. But I get out. My CPS worker comes and gets me, brings me to a foster home in Renton. My foster mom's name was Kristen. I'm living there. I do good my first month out. I aint getting in no trouble. I'm going to school. I aint running around doing the shit I used to do. Just kickin it. But around November, like the middle of November, I started to mess up. I start smoking weed.

I take off from the foster home. I was stealing, selling dope. Just a bunch of the same shit I was doing when I was out before going to Echo Glen. I ran from the foster home like 6 times. I don't know why, it was the best one I'd been to out of all the foster homes I'd been to. And I had to fuck it all up. I mean, I fucked the foster home up pretty bad too. I stole from them, I was a bad influence on every kid and teenager there. I treated a girl there like shit. Just because there was no reason, I just used her for sex. I was just fucking shit up.

On New Year's is when I really fucked up. I ran away again, go up to Muckleshoot, get messed up. Kristen comes and gets me on New Year's Day. I go home, take a shower, clean up, and I leave again. I go back to Auburn and I meet up with the little homie Rob. We do some dumb shit. We steal some cars, sell dope, rob some people, just some stupid shit I wish I didn't do. We get locked up on 1-5-99 for a TMV (Taking a Motor Vehicle), wait there for 72 hours to see if anyone is going to press charges. They do. I go to court, and they said I could get out and come back to court. I got out the 15th, ten days later. I was s'posed to got to court, but the day before, I take off. I went to Aberdeen and there I started drinking, and I caught up with my cuzin Nish. I just got drunk all that day and night, and I didn't stop but to sleep. The next day we started right back up again. When I woke up we was back in Aberdeen, and I was walking down the streets trying to steal a car or something.

Well, I got in a Jeep Grand Cherokee and some lady came out and said -What are you doing in my car? And I jumped out and beat the hell out of her, cause she scared me. She started to hand her money over to me, and I took it, left. I went to the pool hall I used to go to when I was little and I seen some old friends, and I said what's up and I left. I went to the bus stop right across the street and I saw some girls I used to know. I was talking to them, talking about what they told me when I was a little kid. They said when I got older they would mess with me.

The cops caught me, and then I was on my way to the police station. I wasn't doing what they wanted me to do so they started to slam me around and kicking, shit like that. After that they put me in a little ass cell for about a hour, then they brought me to the hospital. So my victim could say yes or no if I was the one who robbed her. Some dude brought me to juvy. I took my shower, got my bedding

,and went to my room. The first three days I didn't know why I was there. My lawyer comes and tells me. I just sit there dumbfounded because before I went and took off I had a dream or a vision or something.

I got locked up and got a lot of time. He told me what I was looking at as a juvenile. I was looking at 5 years. Then he told me they was going to try me as an adult. The next day I go to county jail, but their wish didn't come true. I sit in juvy for three months before they do anything besides try to send me to County. I went to court on April 1, 1999, and the judge said I was gonna get till I was 21, which was 5 years. But I took a plea bargain and got 3 years 8 months.

On April 6, 1999 they sent me to Maple Lane School. I was here for about a week and then I went to court in King County for the TMV and they told me to come back. They shipped me back to the Lane, and when I came back they put me in an open campus cottage. I was in that cottage for about a week, and I went back to the King County for court. They tried to give me two years for the TMV, but my lawyer said she thought what was too much cause I already have almost 4 years. So they just gave me 30 days. I sat in King County about 2 weeks and then I got a phone call from my foster mom. She was talking to me for a little bit. I don't remember what she was saying, but one thing she asked me was how I was feeling.

I don't remember what time this was, but it was May 18, 1999. That night there was a chaplin there, and I asked him to pray for my mama and then we went to the gym. The staff Debbie came over and told me we had to go back to another hall. She told me I was going back to the Lane and she was telling me she wishes me the best, and I get to intake and the staff from the Lane was waiting for me. He tells me my mama's dead, and I really didn't know what to do. I wasn't trying to go off cause I was trying to do what my mama wants me to do. Cause me and my mama wasn't that close, and I didn't do what she wanted me to do so I'm just gonna do it for her now cause I know she's in heaven watching me. We wasn't that close cause I aint seen her for so long.

The staff from Maple Lane was at King County to bring me to the hospital to see my mom alive for the last time. I guess they had her on a life machine till I got there. Well, we got there and I really didn't know whether to cry or hold it all in, so I did what I thought would be good for me in the future. I cried and talked with my family and my foster mom. At 12 am we left cause I guess that's when they pull the plug, and my family didn't want me there when they did that.

We got back to Maple Lane about 2 or 2:30 and I guess they told my roommate John about what happened. He gave me love and support. On the 21st of May '99 I went to her funeral and I seen a bunch of family I aint seen in years. I seen my dad for the first time in four years. It felt pretty good. He showed love for me and my mom by comin. That day I ate deer, elk, whale meat, cake, pie, soup, all that good NATIVE food. We had to leave at 3:00pm. I said my good-byes and we was on our way back to Maple Lane. After we got back they had me on suicidal watch for about 3 days. I couldn't do shit without staff being there. After that it was pretty good. I had a lot of support from my caseworker and from other people.

Conclusions from the inside

The feeling of being locked up sucks cause you aint in control of your life no more. You have to do what the staff tells you to do. You have to shit, sleep, and eat when the staff tell you to. Incarceration aint easy cause you lose a lot of your rights you had when you was free. Like being able to take a shower when you want and as long as you want. You lose going to bed when you want, can't eat what you want, and you have to deal with the staff and all your peers around you. That aint that easy. There's a lot of feelings being locked up. You get stressed out, lonely, and the most feeling I have is being mad cause I don't have control of my life, and that feeling brings in the sad feeling cause I'm sad cause I have to do what the staff tell me to do. Sad cause my family is so far away. And I get mad cause they don't come to see me cause it's my fault that I'm in here.

It's not fun. In some places you're just a number. Some people like me can only talk to their families and friends on the phone cause they're poor and don't have a car or money to come see you or they just live on the other side of the state. Me, my family, they're not poor, but they aint rich. My sister, she has to pay child support. My mom died when I was here at Maple Lane. But when I was in Echo Glen, I told her not to come visit cause I didn't want her to see me in this kind of place even if she knew what it was like. It aint easy seeing your family leave and you not being able to go with them. My dad, it's a little easier for him to come see me, but then again it aint. Cause he lives way up by Canada. He lives in Neah Bay, but he comes to see me when he can or if he's around this part of Washington.

To me bein' locked up is good in ways, but then you got those days when you just dwell on what you did to come here or come back. I didn't have no feeling the first time I got sent up, but this time I got a lot of feelings. I got a kid now. I got a female out there I want to be with. I think about my life and what I want to go do with it. I know what I want to do with it now. I'm tired of this troubled life I lived. It didn't get me nowhere. It only got me what I wanted at the time, and later, it made me pay for it, and not with money. It made me pay for it with 6 years of my life. I didn't really have a chance to be a kid except that one year at my brother John's house, and that wasn't enough.

I didn't write that much about fun stuff I did or I didn't write anything about me bein' good as a child. It's because there wasn't any or I just don't remember. I hope it's that I just don't remember. Right now I do good because I pretty much have to. If I do bad, that aint gonna get me out, and you gotta start doin' good somewhere.

I know a lot of people are gonna think I need to stay locked up my whole life, and maybe I do. But they got to look at what I'm doing now. They got to understand that I want to change my life around. I aint happy for all the stuff I done. I aint happy cause I had to sell dope to be able to eat or do any of that stuff I had done. I aint happy because I treated my girls bad. But people are gonna have to understand that my people aint the ones that brought this stuff. My people were happy the way they was. Then drugs, alcohol, guns, all kinds of stuff was brought over here by whites. And now the white people want to judge us because we use it or do it. I don't think that's cool. But that's life and I can't do shit about it. I can only listen to it and see it. I can show the young kids and the ones that never been off the rez that there's a better life than that life full of hate and drugs and gangs. Let them know that I been through what they're gonna face when they get older or when they leave the rez.

A PRISON CALLED THE MIND

JOHN PAUL

I listened to country music, went to rodeos with my family, wore cowboy boots, the whole nine yards. For the most part, people saw me as a happy little boy. But if any of those people took a look at what really went on, they would probably be shocked.

Hey... Let me introduce myself. My name's John, and I was in Maple Lane School for about 19 months, on assault and drug charges.

This is the story of what I remember of my life. A lot of things in this story had to be skipped, because I have most of the past blocked out of my mind. Everything in the story is true, and almost everything in this story had a major impact on my life. I'm not going to ask that you enjoy the story, because it's not something that someone would normally enjoy. There are some parts that are pretty disturbing, so if you have a weak stomach, you should keep that in mind.

Chapter One: Fear

I was born into a pretty sheltered life, you know. I didn't understand politics until I was about 16, I was pretty much only concerned with what happened to me, and the world was too big of a place to keep track of. Besides, who needs politics when you have a Nintendo at home?

I was born in Shelton, WA on July 25, 1982. Raised until I was 14 by a single mother of 6 children. I am also the only one in my family with no siblings by the same father. The siblings I have always thought that my mom treated me better than them, that I was spoiled, I always got what I wanted, and that she loved me more than them. Which I think is why the abuse started.

I don't remember much until I was in second grade, and at that time, we lived in Amarillo, TX. I adapted to the country-southern lifestyle pretty quickly. I listened to country music, went to rodeos with my family, wore cowboy boots, the whole nine yards. For the most part, people saw me as a happy little boy. But if any of those people took a look at what really went on, they would probably be shocked.

At random points in time, everyday for about 12 years, I would be punched, kicked, beaten, hit with different objects, suffocated, cut, and emotionally tortured. Every chance that one of my siblings could get, when Mom wasn't looking or was at work, they would give me everything they had. My life at that point in time was utter hell, and my mind decided that it couldn't deal with it. So, I ended up locking my emotions, feelings, and fear behind a door in the back of my mind. I wouldn't retrieve the key for another 12 years.

It was about that time that my mother bought a piano. We had a small house, but it fit nicely in the dining room. Nobody ever really played it, though, which made me wonder why we had it. There was sheet music on it, but it gathered more dust than anything did. So, I decided that I would start pushing keys. At first, it was just a one-finger job. I would hear a commercial for, say, a soft drink of some sort, and I would plunk out the notes to the jingle. The sheet music was too complicated for me, so instead I only played what I heard on TV.

After a while, my siblings decided they were getting annoyed with my playing and would force me to stop. Oftentimes, I would be so emotionally numb to everything that I didn't care if I got beat while on the piano bench, because dammit, I wanted to play it! Eventually I would only play when no one was around, or when my mother was there to keep me from getting hurt.

My school life in elementary wasn't much better. I hid the life I had at home inside, and ironically it showed. I was always avoiding questions about home life, and I didn't really have any friends. I was afraid to have anyone from class come over to my house, and I wasn't really allowed to hang out after school. I was made fun of for the most part, and eventually I started to lash out at people.

From that point, I knew the principal quite well, as I would be sent there pretty frequently from class. Back then, the law allowed for the principal or assistant principal to give bad kids spankings with a paddle. For the most part, I would be purposely sent from class to avoid being made fun of. The spankings weren't too bad, and hell, I definitely had worse at home, so there wasn't much for me to lose. My teachers seemed to know that something was wrong in my life, but they couldn't exactly pinpoint it. All of my teachers were really nice to me, even if I wasn't to them. Even the principal seemed to cringe when I came in his office.

Well, one day, I was late for school, and one of my siblings was mad at me for something. They figured my being late was a great excuse to kick my ass, even though they really gave a damn less how late I was. They went into the closet, grabbed a metal wire coat hanger, and tackled me. I was hit on the chest, face, head, everywhere. When I went to school, I had to go to the office, which was policy when you were tardy. When I walked in, all eyes were on me. My eyes were blackened, my face bruised, and my nose was bleeding. When they asked me what had happened, I couldn't speak. I didn't really know what was going on, and I was too numb to care. They assumed it was my mother, and they ended up calling child protective services. My mother was accused of beating me, and we were forced to move back to Washington to avoid me being taken away and my mother going to trial.

Then, it got even worse. My family blamed the whole situation on me, which gave them a really good excuse to kick my ass even worse. It went far beyond a simple ass kicking at times, but they learned not to hit me in the face. I bruised easily, and they didn't want anything to show that they did it. My mother gave the piano away, and we drove through the western coast to Tacoma. We made stops on the way, we had some fun, but when it was over and we were in Washington, it all started again. This time, they didn't care if Mom was in the room, or standing right next to me. They would just nonchalantly walk by, punch me in the chest, and walk away. From there on, I remember only certain spurts in time, and it was about then that I lost hold on my sanity.

Chapter Two: Hate

After living in Tacoma for a few months, we moved to Olympia, WA. It was definitely a change in scenery, and it didn't smell nearly as bad. I pretty much automatically liked Olympia. I went to a local elementary school, and my grades started to come back up. My family didn't fuck with me as much, but I didn't really care. I was so emotionally sick of them that I could have cared less if they were shot. I had two faces, though. On one, I wanted them to die. On the other, I pretended to be somewhat happy. I played it off pretty well for the most part; I had my entire life to learn how to try and manipulate.

When I went into the fifth grade, I got my first skateboard, got back into the piano at my school, and took my first hit of weed. Pretty much, a friend of mine came over, and invited me to his house. He asked me if I smoked weed, which I didn't and said so. He asked me if I wanted to, I said sure. So, we smoked some really horrible stuff, but I still got pretty stoned.

I went home, and somehow my mother found out. Ow.

Well, eventually we moved to Lacey for some reason or other, and I went to middle school there. 6th grade was horrible. I was a total geek by everybody's standards, and I had almost no friends . . . again. It was a bit worse than elementary. Only this time, the beatings didn't really happen that much, and I felt safe to bring over friends.

Somewhere halfway through 6th grade, my mother and I got into an argument about something. I got pissed off and told her I was going to run away from home. And I did. About an hour later, I grabbed some clothes and left.

I wandered around downtown Olympia for about a week, doing more and more drugs as I went along, and then decided to go back home. I was starting to hang out with the "wrong" crowd, but hey, at least they didn't clown on me and hit me with shit. For a while, there even seemed to be a pseudo-love for the "street family."

When I came home, my mom was in tears, and my family blamed and hated me . . . once again. So, I said fuck it, and left for about six months this time, leaving no room in my mind for remorse or regret.

Chapter Three: Self Destruct

I ended up moving in with a friend in the west-side area of Olympia. I got really heavy into crank (Methamphetamines), and by my 13th birthday, I was selling full-time. All day, the only thing I did was sell meth to people two to four times my age. I weighed about 85 pounds, and I was about 5'9". I looked really pathetic. I was so skinny that one would think that I would fly off if the wind blew too hard.

After a while, I decided that being a runaway was lame, so I went home. My whole family didn't even really talk to me, but my mom was just glad that I was home. So, I decided to stay for a while. We lived in the trailer for a little while more, and we moved again.

This time, we moved a little further out in Lacey. I was a total social butterfly by then, so within about three weeks, I had a whole new crowd a friends, and a girlfriend. I was enrolled at a local school, even though I skipped most of the time. I was starting to really get into trouble with things. I was doing more and more drugs . . . again.

My first run-in with the law happened about two months later. A friend of mine and I decided we were bored and burned down a house. I admitted to it later and was charged with 1st degree reckless burning. I was sentenced to a year of probation.

Well, I never really got off of probation, because I was always in violation of it for some reason or another, and every violation means another. I started to get into "Industrial" music, and I also got into masochism. I would cut myself randomly, just because it felt good. I would take extreme, unnecessary risks. I didn't really care about my life. I figured that nothing really mattered that much to me, so fuck it. Life's a risk anyway. Why not make a few more?

At this point I decided that I couldn't take much more of the law and my family, so I ran away again. This is one of the things that I really wish I hadn't done. One day, I was in downtown Olympia, and I had smoked some weed. A man saw me asking people for spare change, and he came over to me and gave me five dollars. He asked me if he could buy me something to eat, and I said sure. Hell-I was starving! We went to a cafe, had food, and he asked me if I drank. I said sure, so we went to his boat on the marina.

As soon as we got on the boat, he punched me on the head, almost knocking me unconcious. He grabbed me, tied my hands up, and threw me on his bed. He unzipped his pants and forced me to give him oral sex. I don't remember anything else from that night. Except when he let me go, I broke a bottle on his head and kicked him in the face several times. I stomped on his testicles, took his wallet, and left.

I was gone from home for about another six months and, once

again, decided to go back home. My aunt and mother came and picked me up downtown, and we went home. My mother brought me in the house, treated me very nicely, wanted to make sure I was OK, asked if I was hungry. The whole motherly thing.

She brought me into room, and sat me down next to her. She gave me a cigarette, and said she had some bad news. I thought it had something to do with the law. It didn't.

My mother had cancer. And she would not live much longer.

I went into my room and thought about it for a while. It didn't really hit me as much as I thought it would, but I became depressed anyway. I was in a state of melancholy for about another year.

Chapter Four: No Place to Run, No Place to Hide

I lived in oblivion for the next couple years. I was in an alcoholic haze everyday and would turn no drug down. I moved out because I figured that my mother couldn't take care of me anymore. I moved into a treehouse in the woods that was in shambles and added a lot of stuff to it. I was cutting myself more and more everyday, my whole arm was covered in scars and old and new cuts. I was gaining a little more weight, but by no means was I healthier.

A couple of years later, I was downtown with my brother, and my mother was in the hospital. We called her, and my sister answered the phone. She said that mom was dying. Joey went somewhere, I'm not sure, but I went to a park downtown, where they were having a fair. I didn't really believe that she would die, so I sat down for a while.

A while later, I took the bus up to the hospital, my mind set on seeing my mother before she died, if she was going to. At the hospital, I took the elevator to her floor, and went to her room. The room was dark, and mom was sleeping. She and I were the only ones there. I walked up to her, and touched her face.

She was dead. My only friend was dead. Forever.

Chapter Five: Angst

After my mother's death, which was less than a week from my birthday, I moved to Shelton, WA. I was barely able to make it to the funeral, I was afraid of what I would have to face. And everything that I had expected to happen happened. Lots of people, tears, depression, and gospel music. After the funeral, I went home and did my daily ritual of butcher knife body art. I guess I cut a little too deep, because I was in the hospital when I woke up.

I ended up moving back into the treehouse for a while, and then I moved into an apartment with some friends. Day in, day out, it seemed like I was doing the same thing everyday. So, my roommates and I started to manufacture drugs. I was getting a little crazier mentally as each day went by, and eventually I cracked. There was a guy at my apartment, he was being belligerent and wouldn't leave, and I ended up cutting his hand with a meat cleaver.

He pressed charges, and when the cops finally arrested me, I had some LSD and weed in my backpack. I was headed up shit creek in a raft with no oars.

Chapter Six: Caged

I went to the Olympia detention center, stayed a month, and was sentenced. When I came to Maple Lane, I, like most everyone else, went to the intake cottage. I was there for about 10 days, then I got crazy on the bullshit medication they were shoving in my system and hung myself with a sock. When they found me, I guess I had quite a few superficial claw marks on the bottom sides of my arms and I bled quite a bit. I don't remember too much of that day, like so many others. Well, I went straight from intake to mental health. Mental health or mental hell, I prefer the latter. It's fitting. I was in mental hell for a month before they released me to the "special" unit. It was not a happy place to be. Everyone in the cottage, about 16 kids, took medication. All of them. And about every other day there was a "code 2" security response because someone had shit all over themselves, their rooms. They would bathe in their urine. They would have conversations with walls. Talk to insects. Talk to their food.

My trip to the mental health cottage was the first of three. It was the same hell all three times. Well, my counselor, we'll call her Jane. She lit up rooms. A real wonderful person. She's one of the few people I don't hate. Maybe, deep down there's a kind of family type of love. See, my mom died a week, actually 6 days before my fifteenth birthday. She left me with kind of a emotional attachment to the maternal type of older woman. When Jane and I first started talking, I kinda knew we had a lot in common. She had been through a lot of the stuff that I had been. We hit it off almost instantly. She had that maternal quality that I had longed for since my own mother died, so in a sense, she kind of took that place. No one, though, can even come close to filling the hole in my heart that belongs to my mother. I still think about her everyday.

On March 5th, my brother (one of four) and my uncle came to visit me. That is the only visit I have received from my family since I came here, and they weren't there to visit me. They came to tell me that my aunt had died. Now I'm not saying my family doesn't love me, they just haven't come to visit me. My uncle came from New York, so I don't think it's a distance thing. To tell you the truth, I don't know at all why they haven't come to see me.

On April Fools Day, I went to a new cottage. This one, you see, is the cottage where the nerds, "issue" kids, underage and socially "unaccepted" kids go. I may have been a nerd, and I was definitely socially "unaccepted." Obviously, because I was there a third of my time, I actually had some fun times there. Back then we had personal stereos in our rooms, which kicked major ass, because I am completely obsessed with music. I didn't have a radio for a while there, and I was on my own with that subject because my family has proved unreliable in mailing me anything, letters included. After awhile, the state provided me with a small cassette player, it was good enough for me because it got the local rock station 107.7, The End. That was my favorite, and I spent a good majority of my time isolating myself in my own little world listening to that station. They don't like it when you isolate yourself here. They don't mind when the guards do it, but when you do it, it's called "Antisocial Behavior" which reeks of consequence. Anything that deviates a norm of society here is deemed "Antisocial" and will be punished.

Anyway, while I was in that cottage, there was a music class at the school. Save for the fact that everything is locked, bathrooms included, it's pretty much just like a regular high school. Anyway, this music class kicked ass. There were two Fender Strats with three single coil pickups, and a Fender P-bass with two of them. There were like nine or ten Yamaha keyboards and a couple acoustic guitars. The teacher also had a set of electric drums but they sucked balls. I wrote quite a few songs, few of which actually had music, but I wrote a lot of lyrics. I'd like to try and get big with my music. I don't know how or when, but I would like to. Actually, I'd love it. I can play all the instruments I named above, with either a small or exceptional amount of talent. I've played piano for about 13 years, guitar for 2, drums for 1. Strangely, I'm just about as good on the drums as I am on the piano.

After I was in that cottage for 6 months, I put in a memorandum to go to one of the work cottages. I started working in the high school as a janitor. I was actually fired soon thereafter, because for one, I'm not that strong and couldn't lift much, and two, I cussed out my boss after he made fun of me. Then I got to work in the dishroom of the Maple Lane cafeteria. Oh, gee that was fun. We get paid $1 an hour, which is actually more than most institutions and prisons, which pay 35 cents an hour. I worked in the dishroom for about a month, then my counselor asked me if I would go to treatment. Seeing no harm, I said I would. There is also a penalty for refusing treatment. You automatically get your maximum release date. So I went to a different cottage. It started out to be okay. I was actually kinda serious about treatment. There was a lot of racism in the work cottage and it kind of followed over into this one. I have black family. I love my family, regardless of color. There were other people who didn't think the same way, and this punk decided to call my nephew and niece pygmies. Which really pissed me off. Then he called them something else, which unless you're naive, you can guess, so I got up and pushed him into his chair. He got up and punched me in the jaw, then staff slammed us both and called a code 2. Security came, and staff told them I was the aggressor, so I had to go to "The Hole." This was my second time going there.

In the "Hole," one of the conditions is the traditional strip search. Now, if there's anything I hate the most, it's strip searches. If you don't consent to a strip search, you don't leave the "Hole." You also don't get out of handcuffs. So I ended up sleeping on the cold concrete floor in my handcuffs and leg irons for three hours. Trying to sleep anyway. It's a little hard when the only air you breathe is contaminated with the scent of human urine and feces. Well, later on, they came and told me that I could leave right away if I strip searched. I told them to rot in hell. Another hour passed, and I eventually grew weary of the game. But I decided that I wouldn't relent without my share of some fun. If they wanted me to strip, I would do just that. I pressed my intercom buzzer and told the faceless voices booming in my room that I would consent. "You're serious?" they inquired. "Well," I said, "if you don't want to believe me I can just sit here and pound on my door and buzz up and annoy you for the rest of your shift."

"Be right there."

Security came, and I stripped, literally. I took my time taking off my shirt, slowly, slowly . . . wow. The look on their faces. Anyway, after my "strip show," they took me back to the cottage, where I could finally rest with some peace.

The rest of my stay in the pre-treatment cottage was sheer, unadulterated hell. I constantly was tormented by residents and staff alike. Finally, one day I couldn't handle it anymore, but instead of hitting a person, I hit the wall. Hard. Regardless of that fact, the wall won. As I walked down the corridor to my cell, I realized I may have broken something. I looked down at my hand. It didn't necessarily hurt, but the entire right side of my right hand was sunken in and my knuckles looked like they were in the middle of my hand. It didn't exactly feel warm and fuzzy. Once I got into my room, I think I went into shock. I got extremely cold and I started screaming and crying. The staff came, saw that my hand was broken and started laughing.

Two hours later I received medical attention which consisted of "Yep, it's broke" and two Ibuprofen.

A half-hour later, they gave me an orange jumpsuit to go off campus. They put a large chain around my waist, which was connected to a handcuff on either side of the hip. Thankfully, they only made me put on the left handcuff. On the way to the hospital, the security officer did nothing but laugh at me. Granted, I shouldn't hit walls, when you do, you take that chance of breaking something. Regardless, it doesn't mean I deserved that kind of treatment.

At the hospital after two hours of waiting, the doctor was actually very kind. He told me the diagnosis - right pinkie and ring medicarpal had snapped in two. He "gently" set the bones into place and gave me a makeshift cast for the time being.

After a month they switched me to the drug treatment program. Let me tell you, I've seen more drugs in the treatment cottage than I have ANYWHERE on campus. I was serious, however, to an extent about treatment. So I didn't do any of the drugs.

I made it two weeks in that cottage before I went looney. I had a shank in my room, and for some reason or other, I decided to die. I made sure there were no staff or residents in my pod area, and I went over to my bed and turned my back to the wall. That was about when I passed out.

When I next looked up, there was blood everywhere. My entire left forearm was covered in blood. There was blood on my clothes. The floor. The wall. The bed. The underside of my left arm had about ten superficial incisions and five or ten threatening ones. It didn't matter, and it didn't hurt. I looked over at the door and there was a staff with a video camera. I don't know how long they were there, but that camera royally pissed me off. I picked up my shank and walked over to the window. I somehow managed to threaten enough to get the camera away and off. I phased out again.

I ended up survivng the incident, but I still have scars.

Chapter Seven: A Fork In the Road

A while later, I was told about the Gateway Program. I had always been fascinated by The Evergreen State College and decided "Why the hell not?" So, since I had recieved my GED the previous month, I enrolled.

It started off kinda rough. I wasn't really used to any sort of college, but it eventually smoothed out. The next quarter, part of the class was set aside to do this book. At first, we had no idea that it would be published, but here it is! When June 1st came along, I had less than a month before my release.

I became really nervous, and I was sure it would be the same as before. But I also thought that I could make it different. Well, I thought, I could always try.

Epilogue: Walking the Path

June 25, 2000 - Well, here I am, released into the world. Everything seems so different. Everything is so . . . changed. Maybe not physically, but I can feel it somehow. It's hard to describe. So, I guess I need to get back home. It's past my parole curfew.

NO EASY ANSWERS
A COLLEGE STUDENT AT MAPLE LANE

STEVE MENTER

There are not many hardships a privileged North Dallas Jewish kid has to face while growing up. Everything I needed was and is always provided for me. Economically, medically, and emotionally, I couldn't have asked for a better childhood. This, however, does not mean that my childhood was easy. In fact, I remember the opposite. I remember loneliness, not fitting in, awkward sexuality, mean Christian friends, drugs, and a lack of general knowledge on how to treat a hyperactive, angry child. Yet with this lonely and confusing childhood I had, how did I graduate high school, and how is it that I am about to graduate from college? The answer is not that easy.

My parents bought me all the shrinks money could buy, they sent me to all the schools for kids with learning 'disabilities,' and when my circus of a high school kicked me out, they sent me to an outpatient rehab ten minutes from my neighborhood in Dallas. So every time I was in trouble, in any way, there was always somebody with the resources to help me out. I was a pretty fortunate person. I knew this, but it never really registered. I never really understood the fact that a lot of people in this country are not as fortunate as I am. I am lucky and grateful for all the people who have put me on the path to doing something with my life. The alternative was, lonely druggie. After years of wondering when I was going to take advantage of my privileges, I finally left Texas for Olympia, Washington and The Evergreen State College.

My first program at Evergreen was a class on the struggles of Indigenous people past and present, and the current revitalization of indigenous cultures throughout the world. Within this program there was an optional workshop, and this workshop was and still is called the Gateway Program.

When I first started going out to Maple Lane, I really had no idea what to expect. I was a little tentative at first, and I had no clue what we were supposed to do. The founder of the program told the Evergreen students not to try and act cool. She also told us to do all the reading and get any cultural information that the Maple Lane Students asked for. I would do some of the reading and pretend in seminar that I did it all. Basically, I was doing what I have always done in school and in life in general. That is - do just enough to get by without anyone knowing.

Towards the middle of the first quarter of school, I noticed a slight change to my approach. I was getting more comfortable in the setting out there. I was starting to know the Evergreen students, as well as the Maple Lane students, better. Most importantly, I was taking this program personally. It's kind of nice to know that I can go in and out of a jail, it's kind of rough to know that some of my peers can't. For maybe the first time in my life, I was starting to look at my privilege. My life was set up very well. This set-up led to my success and my lack of hardships. I have full advantage over many people in this world. That knocked me on my ass.

The Gateway Program got a little easier to understand. It is not about the Evergreen students going to tell these "delinquent" youth how to live their lives. They get enough of that while locked up. The Gateway Program is about equality and hope and empowerment. We go there to learn. It does not take long to find out that the majority of these kids are bright. In seminar, they consistently make us college students question our own beliefs and ideas. However, to most of these youths, college is not an option. It is not something that is considered often. Plus, the State of Washington makes education and rehabilitation very hard to come by. The Gateway Program fills the gap between the privileged and the have-nots. We, the white college students with middle-class parents, should go into prisons and work with prisoners. We should go because we have the privilege to go. By acting on our privilege, we help make things more equal. We learn, the Maple Lane students learn and have a chance to have fun, and smiles come to young adults who don't smile and definitely don't have fun.

Do I now know what to do and say every Tuesday when I make my journey to Maple Lane? No, actually, I do not. That is really not important. What's important is that I go out there and be myself (whatever that means) and put time and energy into creating a cooperative learning environment. The seminars and workshops at Maple Lane are more interesting, more meaningful, more creative, and more comfortable than the seminars at Evergreen. The level of comfort grows and as that grows, the commitment grows.

The process of starting to treasure and get involved in Gateway led to many experiences that I surely would have never had. First, I got to meet my privilege and my history face to face. Then I got to know and learn with young men that I was not expecting to know and learn with. Then in spring quarter, my friend and classmate, Matt Walsh, and I got to lead a separate class every Wednesday at nine o'clock in the morning.

A few of the Maple Lane students wanted to do more, so we did. For the first time in my life I was faced with real academic responsibility. I had to be prepared and willing. Matt and I had to come up with a course of study. We decided to read and have seminar over *Cold New World* by the journalist William Finnegan. This book consists of four stories about poverty, youth, drugs, and violence in different parts of this often-times cold country. The response to this book was enthusiastic. The seminars were happening and we were developing something of a bond. We finished the book. Now the Maple Lane students were to write their own stories in their own language.

A journalist wrote *Cold New World*. It was in his voice. Yet, where is the voice of the youth in this world? Where are the voices of incarcerated youth? The only voice out there for youth is politicians, lawmakers, parents, journalists, and the police. We wanted something different, plus it's always positive to write your life down. So all eight Maple Lane students wrote their own stories. These stories make up this book. The only credit I deserve for this book is that I went out there. I showed up when most people don't. I did nothing to help these young men improve there lives or to become better writers. All I did was believe that they are capable and let them do the rest. This class was the most special academic experience I have ever had.

This experience of being involved with Gateway has done a lot. It has made my own life easier to understand. I want to delve deeper and deeper into programs like this one, and maybe set some more up. I want to look at my own situation and see what I can do about it. This experience has also made me frustrated. The fact is that the system we live in is only set up for certain people. For everyone else it is rigged. That sounds simple, I know. Yet, look at who spends the most time in prison. Look at why some people serve longer sentences for the same exact crime. Look at where most of the money is. You will find inequality, racism, and lies. Why? Well, because it benefits the people on top and because it puts power into the hands of few.

Throughout my life I have felt inadequate, Jewish, wealthy, confused, lonely, and smart. It is difficult to piece things together and to understand life and the emotions we face everyday. It is especially difficult to understand and make sense out of the juvenile justice system, the inner-self, and the state of the world. Yet, it seems that all these things are colliding together right now. It's a beautiful collision in a new and strange way. A lot of times I would like to go back to doing nothing with my life. I can turn on the television, eat some chocolate, and put substances in me. This would be very easy, and I am very capable of doing what is easy. I did what is easy for a long time. However, I think I will continue to investigate my life, stay aware of my privilege, and act upon that awareness.

BREAKING DOWN THE MYTHS
TEEN CRIME IN THE USA

JULIA ALLEN

The media portrays youth as gangsters who are violent and are always up to no good, and audiences often believe what the media portrays. The nasty image of teens as dangerous punks who don't care about anything, follows us. . . wherever we go. When this . . . offensive image follows teens into [our] own schools, the positive learning environment crumbles and criminalization of youth begins. Adults have to understand that youth aren't always negative, and if you cage us up, we'll start to act like animals. But if you nurture us, we'll be able to succeed further in life.

James Lee, 16 years old Oakland, California

This piece is about the myths of youth violence in our country. It's about the role of the media, the politicians, and the prison industry in selling a picture of youth today as lacking all morals, corrupted to the core. It's about the reality of decreasing crime stats, and putting the school shootings back into perspective. It's about the militarization of our schools, where young people are being treated as suspects before students. And it's about the racism at large in the Juvenile Justice system, how that manifests on the streets, in the gang laws, and in the unequal sentencing of youth of color.

Having heard the stories of these eight young men, a reader will notice that each of them come from single parent homes or working class neighborhoods or immigrant families. Some have lived through severe domestic abuse and seven out of eight of them are young people of color. The truth is, their backgrounds are similar to nearly all of the incarcerated youth in our country today, and this is not by accident.

Part I : The Myth and Who's Behind It

The Juvenile court was created in 1899. It was "founded on the belief that children were entitled to a range of special protections due to their vulnerability and immaturity, the juvenile court was intended to separate youth from the [harmful] effects of the adult justice system."[1]

Fundamental to the juvenile court was the belief that youth offenders could still change. But in the past 10 years, general opinion about this "vulnerability" has been replaced with other views. Fueled by the school shootings and the increase of youth who've got access to guns, the media and the politicians have launched a campaign to turn teenagers into a national enemy. Television tells parents to fear their own children, calling them "ticking time bombs" and "adolescent super-predators." It tells us we're in the midst of a "teenage crime storm," "a tidal wave" of total violence. Young people have become criminal for every aspect of who they are; their music, clothes, language, and relationships. They are suspects in their own schools, on the streets, and everywhere else.

Media

"Headline-grabbing youth crimes account for less than 1% of all juvenile delinquency"[2] and the juvenile homicide rate went down 56% between 1993-1998.[3] That means prime time TV is really having to stretch the stories of youth violence in order to make it seem like there's a "crime storm" growing stronger by the day. And as for the recent school killings, which are "sweeping the nation," an "epidemic" beyond control, a student in the U.S. has a 1 in a million chance of getting killed at school. You're twice as likely to get struck by lightning and die from that.[4]

But in recent studies and phone polls, paranoia about youth violence seems to be at an all time high. In a nationwide poll 62% of the people thought that juvenile crime was increasing, and according to CBS news, 80% of Americans "expect more school shootings."[5] People are listening to their televisions. It's dangerous when the mainstream media is our only way of getting information. It shapes our idea of reality.

Why would we be told youth violence is sweeping the nation and only getting worse, if it's not true?

1) Prisons

Youth violence peaked out in 1993; since then, all major crime rates have been dropping. That includes rape, robbery, aggravated assault, and homicide. Each of these dropped by at least 27% since 1993.[6] Youth crime, like adult crime, has stayed basically stable or gone down over the past 20 years, even though the amount of people being arrested and the amount of prisons being built to house them, contain them, is growing all the time. The US is experiencing the biggest prison build-up in our history, the most people locked-up out of any country in the Western world, with no sign of slowing.

The "budget for the California Dept. of Corrections will grow from $3.5 billion to nearly $5 billion by the year 2000. In order to keep pace with the incarceration rate, 24 new prisons will need to be built by 2005."[7] Prison guard unions are getting to be very powerful. With their jobs on the line, more people and families are going to be invested in the prison build-up. California's prison guard union was the state's biggest donor by three times to the last governor, Pete Wilson, who was governor when some of the harshest criminal legislation in the country was pushed through.[8]

Nationwide, "once a prison is built, the state will fill it with an increasing number of nonviolent offenders because there are simply not enough violent offenders to fill the cells."[9] Violent crimes are dropping, prisons are being built up all over the country, and youth are a population that can fill some of those empty cells.

2) Money

The priorities of our country can be seen in the way we spend our money. From 1984 to 1992 spending per $1000 of the average tax-payer's money, went up 47% for corrections (prisons) but just 0.8% for universities and community colleges.[10]

There is a direct relationship between the increase in dollars for the prison build-up and the decrease in funding for education and after-school programs. James Lee of Oakland, California, 16 years old, says: "With increased security and police on campus it seems as if Oakland has given up on the students . . . I can't even ask my teacher for an extra sheet of paper to write on . . . in one of my classes, I can't even take the textbooks home because they can't afford to buy a class set for everyone. Yet the district has funding to send more and more new security personnel to Oakland campuses and maintain the surveillance cameras."[11] He talks about overcrowding and no heat in the winter months while the Oakland school board recently voted to spend $1.13 million a year to have its own 24-hour police force.[12]

We're looking at a serious misdirection of resources. Violence among young people is a problem. But by operating under the opinion that youth are going to be violent, that it cannot be helped, only restricted and punished, we invest our money in the growth of the problem. To create a true, long-lasting solution we would have to deal with the circumstances that create the problem, the environment youth are living in. Instead we leave the circumstances as they are, and the future of youth crime and violence becomes a secure investment.

3) Politicians

Politicians give the official word on how great a threat young people pose to the country. They respond to the paranoia stirred up by the media, they promise us they will do their best to "cure this crisis of youth violence." We have them to thank for such slogans as: "adult crime, adult time." Their policies reflect the attitude of punishment over rehabilitation, using mandatory minimum laws and 3-strikes-you're-out laws on juveniles. Furthering their own careers, politicians have pushed criminal justice reform bills that fundamentally change the human rights of young people.

A bill in Texas says 11 year-olds who commit serious crimes could be given the death penalty. It's sponsored by state senator James Pitts. He says: "Current Juvenile laws could not have anticipated violent crimes being committed by children this young." But there were 25 homicides committed by youth under 13 years old in 1965 and in 1996 there were 13.[13] Homicide arrests of youth under 12 dropped from 41 to 22 from 1993 to 1998.[14] His argument is not true.

Representative Bill McCollum sponsored the "Juvenile Crime Control Act of 1997," originally called the Superpredator Incapacitation Act. McCollum is a Republican from Florida, who has said, among other things: Today's youths "are the most dangerous criminals on the face of the Earth."[15] And "The really bad news" is "America will experience a 31% increase in teenagers."[16]

His bill furthers the nationwide process of dismantling the basics of the juvenile court system: confidentiality, treatment or rehab over lock-up, placing the youth's crime in the context of their lives and their age. His bill offers $1.5 billion in federal money over three years to states that agree to prosecute juvenile offenders as young as 13 as adults.[17] States take this money and expand their facilities only to find themselves further in debt because the prison industry has proven very little return. Using scare tactics, media hype, and the image of bloodthirsty children "running wild in the streets," McCollum's bill passed in the House, 286 to 132.[18]

So, Prisons, Money, and Politicians are three reasons why the media would want to convince us that crime by youth is rising like a tidal wave and we should all be afraid. There's a great deal of investment in the criminalization of young people: money, jobs, new construction, and profit to be had. Fear sells.

Part II : Youth as Targets

"As I see more cops in my school, I think more about what it would be like in jail . . . When I look at a campus cop, I imagine that he sees in me a delinquent who is not going anywhere in life. My self-esteem lowers and I start to see what he sees."-James Lee[19]

Youth are criminalized, they're treated as suspect and dangerous and considered untrustworthy by authorities, based on the fact of their age. Youth who grow up working class or in poverty are especially criminalized. A young person of color who also happens to be poor is like the bull's eye on the target. Brown-skinned, 15, no cash, and you're a criminal who just hasn't committed a crime yet.

Targeted for Class and Race

"It is politically easier to scapegoat teens than to do something about the alarming number of American kids that are growing up in poverty. Of the more than 40 million Americans that live below the federal poverty line, half of them are children and 60% are non-white."[20]

Pointing fingers at youth or gangs as though any violence just springs from them, for no reason and out of context, is a lot easier than looking at the conditions youth and families live in and examining why those conditions can lead to crimes of survival.

Consider women and crimes of survival. Since 1980, the number of women imprisoned in the country has tripled. Most are locked-up for "economic crimes," like check forgery, illegal use of credit cards, and property crimes. 80% of women in prison report incomes of less than $2,000 per year in the year before their arrest, and 92% report incomes under $10,000.[21] Almost two-thirds of women in prison are women of color.[22]

In Washington State, the government released a report, saying youth of color were over-represented in the system because of reasons including "various disadvantaging socio-economic factors."[23] It's no secret that a person's race and class seriously affects how they are prosecuted and how they are sentenced.

The Juvenile Rehabilitation Administration (JRA) in Washington, which runs Maple Lane and other facilities and group homes in the state, says, as of 1998: "Approximately 82 percent of youth committed to JRA are substance abusers or are chemically dependent. The typical youth is two academic years behind his/her peer group. Nearly half of these youth have an essential need for mental health treatment."[24]

The program director of a girl's medium-maximum "holding facility" in Washington says: approximately 95% of the girls have been sexually abused, and if you add physical abuse, she says, it's closer to 100%.[25]

Young offenders here in Washington live through poverty, physical abuse, and sexual abuse. They are neglected by the school system and use drugs to escape. These conditions have been punishment enough for a young life. They warrant a more sympathetic intervention on the part of adults in authority besides incarceration. But these are the young people who fill the cells of our country, punished for what they have been born into and for what they were able to survive.

Targets in the Schools

In the past 15 years and especially since the highly publicized school shootings of the 90's, elementary and high schools across the country have changed their approach to discipline and safety. The focus has shifted from security measures to make students feel comfortable and protect them from outsiders, to security that monitors the students themselves. The reality of youth who carry guns and knives for their own protection exists. The need to secure students' safety while at school is a concern, but the politicians, school officials, and criminal justice system are on the offensive. Students are targeted for their dress styles, behavior, and race. The priority is not the well-being of the student body. The priority is to spot criminals before they commit a crime. As a possible suspect, this fundamentally changes the way young people experience their school environment, and it changes what can be done to them in the name of campus security.

1) **Security:** Parents and school boards, state government, and

the U.S. government are all on board for more metal detectors, locker searches, and student identification badges. Some schools now have their own 24-hour police officers and narcotic police officers, some have video cameras in the buildings, lock-in when school starts, escorts to go to the bathroom, and mandatory mesh book bags. Students say they feel less safe and report more crime in schools that use these "secure" school methods.[26]

Treated as a criminal population, they're monitored, policed, their personal items are searched, they're considered a threat to themselves, others, and teachers. Nearly every state has passed laws that require schools to share information about students with the courts. Kids are sent to the police department instead of the principal's office. They're being tried, arrested, convicted on nothing but talk, threats, gossip, name calling and for being considered "dark", depressed, or angry.[27]

2) Databases: If there has been no evidence against a youth then officials can just turn to the FBI database for how to detect signs of a future school killer:

-trouble with parents
-dislike popular students
-have a break-up or have troubles in a relationship
-listen to songs that have violent words in them

This is the official list and even though it describes at least half of the high school age population, it's being taken seriously. At least 20 schools in the country use a computer profiling system to keep track of the students and "assess" their "level of threat."[28]

3) Suspension: In one year in this country (1997), 3.1 million kids are suspended from school, almost all of them for non-violent and non-criminal offenses. As a rule, students of color are over-represented in the school disciplinary cases everywhere from Providence, Rhode Island to San Francisco, California. Nationwide, black male students tend to be suspended at a rate close to double their population and many of them for "subjectively defined offenses" meaning offenses defined by the person who was there. So instead of being suspended for "fighting" and "physical assault" or even for cheating on tests or schoolwork, they're suspended for things like "disrespect" and "defiance of authority." The race of the teacher, the racism of the school district, the racism of the state, should all be examined, if "defiance of authority" is an offense that will result in the suspension of a student, which is a punishment that has long term effects. Students who are suspended from school are at least three times more likely to drop out altogether. And kids being "excluded from schools are winding up directly in the juvenile justice system."[29]

Where else is there to go?

Targets on the Street

In a time of anti-loitering laws, truancy laws, anti-cruising laws, and curfews, there's little or no options for where young people can just be or go, to relax, socialize, or do something that empowers them. We arrest young people for curfew violations and loitering at 65 times the rate we do for homicides. In the past three years, homicide arrests went down 30%, rape arrests went down 15% and curfew and loitering arrests went up 116%.[30] That means youth are being picked up by the cops for standing around, for sitting somewhere, for having nowhere else to go.

Gang laws specifically target people of color. California's Proposition 21, "The Gang Violence and Juvenile Crime Prevention Act" that passed into law in March 2000, defines a "criminal street gang" as a formal or informal group of three or more people with a common symbol. That means three guys standing together in California wearing the same designer T-shirt could be considered a gang.

However, "The 'gang label' has everything to do with race. . . Frankly, we do not believe that this tactic would have spread so widely and come to be accepted within law enforcement generally, if it was not being applied almost exclusively to people of color," said John Crew of California's ACLU (American Civil Liberties Union). So, it won't be three white boys standing on a curb that'll call the attention of the cops.

As Prop. 21 says in its introduction: "Gang-related crimes pose a unique threat to the public because of gang members' organization and solidarity." It is the presence of young people of color getting organized and getting strong together that is the true threat. It is inner-city Black or Latino or Asian youth in a group, not battling between gangs, but turning their "organization and solidarity" outward to face the cities they live in, to face the "public" who keeps them there, that is the threat.

Gang Databases/Gang Sweeps: Gang databases gather "intelligence" like personal information and photographs of youth. They are listed based on their families, clothing styles, language, tattoos, and haircuts. They are catalogued without evidence of an actual crime. The database in California has 300,000 names and has been used as a model for databases now set up all over the country. "In at least five states, wearing baggy FUBU jeans and being related to a gang member is enough to meet the 'gang member' definition." In Denver, the gang database was exposed as listing eight out of every ten youth of color in the entire city. In Chicago in 1992, an anti-gang loitering ordinance said it was illegal to stand on the street if you were identified as a gang member. But it was also illegal to stand beside somebody cops "reasonably believed" was a gang member. 43,000 youth were arrested under this ordinance in just two years.[31]

Gang databases and gang sweeps, mass arrests and ongoing harassment of could-be gang members have been justified as a way to diffuse the gang war. Youth of color are consistently targeted by the police across this country and, in most cities, arrested at rates way above their population, gang war or no gang war.

Targets in the System

In this country, 68% of the juvenile population is white but 63% of youth in custody are youth of color.[32] There is racism in the juvenile justice system, at every stage of the system.

Let's say a 15-year-old black male youth is arrested, and so is a white 15-year-old. Both are picked-up for the same kind of offense and both have priors. According to the data from at least 17 states, the black youth is more likely to be "petitioned to court, to be detained, and to be placed outside of the home."[33] Youth of color in general are given much harsher sentences with longer time to serve, and they serve it in institutions, not residential facilities. Many states have released reports that speak to the undeniable differences in the treatment of youth of color in their systems.

Washington State: An official government report says, "Minorities appeared to be at greater risk for being charged with more serious offenses than Whites involved in comparable levels of delinquent behavior . . . [resulting] in higher incarceration rates among minorities." That means when a white kid and a Native American kid stand trial for the same offense, files equally thick, the young person of color is charged with a more serious crime. The report says: "African- American youth were particularly more likely to be detained" before going to trial, "formally prosecuted, and [found] guilty than other racial or ethnic groups."[34]

Youth of color are:

California-	53.4% of the youth population **70% of imprisoned youth**
Ohio-	14.3% of the youth population 30% of youth arrested **43% of imprisoned youth**
Texas-	50% of the youth population **80% of imprisoned youth**

In L.A. County ('96) youth of color were **seven times** more likely sent to prison than whites. In New Orleans, LA, African-American youth are arrested at **19 times** the rate of whites.[35]

Juvenile to Adult Court Transfers: All 50 states allow for the transfer of youth to adult court but in the past six years 43 states have passed legislation that makes it easier. 41 states try children as young as 12 in adult court.[36] The young person who gets transferred generally receives much longer time, with the possibility of being sentenced to the death penalty or life without parole. Young people of color are sent to adult court at far greater rates than white youth and often find themselves there for non-violent offenses like property and drug violations. As of 1996, young people of color were 95% of the juvenile to adult court transfers in L.A., and 100% of the juvenile to adult court transfers in Texas.[37] And though states have different laws about where youth are sent to serve their time, youth who are placed in adult facilities are more likely to be violently attacked by staff, they're five times more likely to be raped, and 7.7 times more likely to kill themselves.[38]

To commit some terrible act of violence is to become an adult in the eyes of the law, as if the capacity to do harm is what defines an adult, not maturity, not life experience, not the ability to reason. It's as if childhood is a privilege, and by shooting a gun, youth lose theirs. After that criminal moment, they gain 10 years and can function like adults in an adult's world. It doesn't make any sense and will do nothing to stop a young person from committing more crimes.

Conclusions

So, youth are targeted for their class and race, for the environment they were born into, for just being the age they are. They are targeted on the streets through a variety of laws, including gang laws, which focus almost exclusively on youth of color. As students, youth are monitored constantly as if they really are the "ticking time bombs" they've been called by the media and politicians. They have to learn under the eye of law enforcement, video cameras, and with the threat of being singled out for their mood, their clothes, or because somebody thinks they show the signs of a could-be killer. Some young people describe their experiences in school now as being more like a training ground for prison than for a life of opportunity.

Within the justice system, youth are also targeted. Youth of color are over-sentenced and over-represented. Youth in general are bumped up to the criminal status of an adult to keep pace with the changing public opinion of what violent youth deserve, and as a result of political pressure and financial rewards to states who prove they are tough on juvenile crime. Young people are caught in a whirlwind that's been whipped up by politics and the media. They feel the bitter results of legislation that's come out of school shootings, built fast to satisfy the public's emotion and need for revenge.

Treating young people like criminals is not a remedy for the violence in this country today. Locking up youth who've been abused or have suffered in poverty or who are drug addicted is not a remedy for the problems we face. And there is no remedy in believing that youth who are caught up in gangs are beyond all hope, in punishing them for trying to survive where they live and the circumstances they live in. If there is true concern for the welfare of young people and youth of color especially, it's going to take considering the issues in a very different light. It's going to take listening to the stories young people tell of who they are, how they got to be that way, what was missing, what can still be saved.

notes

1 Males Ph.D., Mike and Macallair MPA, Dan. "The Color of Justice: An Analysis of Juvenile Court Transfers in California." The Justice Policy Institute; Center on Juvenile Crime and Justice (CJCJ), February 2000.

2 Schiraldi, Vincent and Ziedenberg, Jason. "Runaway Juvenile Crime?: The Context of Juvenile Arrests in America." The Justice Policy Institute; CJCJ, March 1998.

3 Donahue, Elizabeth; Schiraldi, Vincent; and Ziedenberg, Jason. "School House Hype: School Shootings and the Real Risks Kids Face in America" and "School House Hype: Two Years Later." The Justice Policy Institute; CJCJ, July 1998, April 2000.

4 "School House Hype," 1998.

5 "School House Hype," 2000.

6 Ibid.

7 Ambrosio, Tara-Jen and Schiraldi, Vincent. "From Classrooms to Cellblocks: A National Perspective." The Justice Policy Institute; CJCJ, February 1997.

8 Ibid.

9 Ibid.

10 Ibid.

11 Lee, James. "Hey, I See the Penitentiary...One Day." Young and Miseducated, a self-published zine from the Asian Pacific Islanders Promoting Advocacy and Leadership, People United for a Better Oakland, and the Korean Community Center. Oakland, California 2000.

12 Pintado-Vertner, Ryan and Chang, Jeff. "The War on Youth." ColorLines Magazine, winter 1999-2000.

13 "School House Hype," 2000.

14 "School House Hype," 1998.

15 "Dispelling the Myth: An Analysis of Youth and Adult Crime Patterns in California over the past 20 years." March 2000.

16 Ayers, William. "The Criminalization of Youth." Rethinking Schools: An Urban Educational Journal. Milwaukee, WI. Winter 1997-98.

17 Reynolds, Morgan O. "The Federal Government and Juvenile Crime." Criminal Justice Center of the National Center for Policy Analysis (NCPA), 2000.

18 U.S. House. "A bill to combat violent youth crime and increase accountability for juvenile criminal offenses," H.R.3, 105th Congress. 1997

19 "Hey I See the Penitentiary...One Day." 2000.

20 Holhut, Randolph T. "Teen Violence: The Myths and Realities." The Written Word, 1996.

An on-line publication- http://www.mdle.com/WrittenWord/rholhut/holhut25.htm

21 "Statistics on the Conditions of Women." Women's Economic Agenda Project, May 1994.

22 De Groot, Anne S. HEPP News, (HIV Education Prison Project), Vol.3 issue 4. Brown University School of Medicine, Providence, Rhode Island, April 2000.

23 Dean Bernard C. "Juvenile Justice and Disproportionality Patterns of Minority Over-representation." Sentencing Guidelines Commission, Olympia, WA, December 1997.

24 "Overview." Washington State Department of Social and Health Services, Juvenile Rehabilitation Administration. December 2, 1998.

25 Eggers, Tiffany Zwicker. "The 'Becca Bill' Would Not Have Saved Becca: Washington State's Treatment of Young Female Offenders." University of Minnesota Law School Journal, American Bar Association Network.

www.abanet.org/crimjust/juvjus/linkgirls.html

26 "School House Hype," 2000.

27 Ibid.

28 Ibid.

29 Ibid.

30 "Runaway Juvenile Crime," 1998.

31 "The War on Youth," winter 1999-2000.

32 Ibid.

33 McGarrell, Edward F. "Juvenile Correctional Reform: Two Decades of Policy and Procedural Change." Clark Boardmen Company, New York, 1994.

34 "Juvenile Justice and Disproportionality Patterns of Minority Over-representation." December 1997.

35 "The Color of Justice," 2000.

36 "The War on Youth," winter 1999-2000.

37 "The Color of Justice," 2000.

38 Schiraldi, Vincent and Ziedenberg, Jason. "The Risks Juveniles Face when they are Incarcerated with Adults." Justice Policy Institute; CJCJ, July 1997.

GLOSSARY OF TERMS

JRA - Juvenile Rehabilitation Administration

Maple Lane and Greenhill - Washington State juvenile maximum security facilities.

Echo Glen - Washington State juvenile facility for female and male residents.

IMU - Intensive Management Unit, "the Hole." Residents are sent to the IMU for major infractions. Standard lockdown procedure is 23-1 which means 23 hours in your cell, 1 hour out. Residents earn time outside their rooms. Current policies do not include 23-1.

Cottages - living unit at juvenile facilities where 20-70 people live. 4-5 staff are on duty at all times.

Group Homes - minimum security house to transition juveniles back to the commuity. 12-15 people live in the homes to work and attend school. Residents also receive therapy here.

Naselle, Mission Creek - group home facilities where Department of Natural Resources offers paid manual labor jobs to juveniles who qualify.

Job Corps - job training at a group home, offers paid apprentice programs to get skills.

TMV - TMVWP - TMVWOOP - Taking a Motor Vehicle (Without Permission, Without Owner's Permission)

Chronic - marijuana

Chillie Pimp - a man who arranges prostitution for only one woman.

Crank - broken down Meth. Mixed often with battery acid and cut 50 times

Crack - cocaine, cooked and rocked up.

C&H - Crack and Heroin

"strap" - carrying a weapon, usually a gun

"juvenile life" - a slang term that refers to a sentence when the resident will not be released until his or her 21st birthday.

ABOUT THE AUTHORS

Julia Allen was born in New York City. She has volunteered with incarcerated youth and women, worked with prison activist organizations, and been an advocate for girls in the system. She is 21 years-old.

Tuan Dang is a true Vietnamese man. He is 20 years young. He's great at everything.

Floyd Gonzalez was born on Spetember 9, 1983 in Seattle, WA. He is Native American from Muckleshoot and Makah nations. He was incarcerated for robbery in the first degree and assualt in the third degree. He was arrested January 27, 1999.

Stephanie Guilloud is a 24 year-old organizer, editor, and writer who lives in Olympia, WA. She edited an anthology of writings written by participants in the 1999 Seattle WTO Protests called *Voices from the WTO*. She has worked in male and female adult prison facilities.

Steven Michael Menter is 22 years-old. He is the son of Jewish immigrants from South Africa who came to Texas in 1976. He attended two community colleges in Dallas, the University of North Texas in Denton, and is currently a student at The Evergreen State College in Olympia, Washington where he will graduate in June of 2001.

Carol J. Minugh is the Gateway Program Director. She is committed to opening doors traditionallly closed to many who would benefit from higher education.

John Paul is 18 years old and attends The Evergreen State College. He is a talented piano player and musician, and he is currently working on an album.

Ben Peters is a member of the Skokomish tribe. He is 18 years-old. He was released in 2000. He is currently unemployed.

Johnathan Dowand Smith is serving 5+ years and will be released when he is 21. He plans to make a difference in his and others' lives. He enjoys rapping, writing, and drawing. He was born in East St. Louis. He currently attends community college.

Chang Saechao is 18 years-old. His release date is November 2001. He is living at a group home and has a job. He is working his way towards freedom.

Simeon Terry was born in Spokane,WA. He is 20 years-old. He is an African-American. He likes playing basketball and he likes nature. He is on his way to finding the truth.

Terrance Turner was incarcerated between the ages of 14 and 21. He is committed to using his experience to benefit others. He is a poet, rap artist, and visual artist.

RESOURCES

Youth Organizations and Youth Writings:

The No War on Youth Online Resources
<www.colorlines.com/waronyouth>

The Beat Within: A Weekly Newsletter of Writing and Art from the Inside
<www.pacificnews.org/yo/beat>

Youth Outlook: The World Through Young People's Eyes
<www.pacificnews.org/yo>

The Progressive Directory youth page, Bay Area groups
<www.emf.net/~cheetham/kyouth-1.html>

BRAT - The Youth Activist Zine
<www.brat.org>

Peer Justice and Youth Empowerment
<www.ncjrs.org/peerhome.htm>

International Student Activism Alliance
<www.studentactivism.org>

Schools Not Jails
<www.schoolsnotjails.com>

Books:

Butterfield, Fox. *All God's Children: the Bosket Family and the American Tradition of Violence.* New York: Knopf, 1998.

The Celling of America. edited by Daniel Burton-Rose, Dan Pens, and Paul Wright. Maine: Common Courage, 1998.

Criminal Injustice. edited by Elihu Rosenblatt. Boston: South End Press, 1996.

Finnegan, William. *Cold New World: Growing up in a Harder Country.* New York: Modern Library, 1999.

Articles and Reports:

Center for Juvenile Crime and Justice (CJCJ) has published a range of reports on criminalization of youth in the U.S. They are available on the web at:
<www.cjcj.org/jpi/publications.html>